2025-2026 EDITION

COLLEGE SOPHOMORE READY

EXPERT ADVICE FOR PARENTS TO NAVIGATE THEIR STUDENT'S SECOND YEAR

EDITED BY
CHELSEA PETREE, Ph.D.

A READY GUIDE

PARENT READY!

PARENT READY

2025–2026 Edition

Copyright © Parent Ready, Inc., 2025

Parent Ready supports the right to free expression and the value of copyright. The purpose of copyright is to encourage the creation of works that enrich our culture.

All rights reserved. No part of this book may be reprinted or reproduced in any form or by any electronic, mechanical, or other means, now known or hereafter invented, including photocopying, recording, and information storage and retrieval, without the prior written permission of the publisher, except in the case of brief quotations embodied in critical articles and reviews.

Published by Parent Ready
8 E. Windsor Avenue
Alexandria, Virginia 22301
https://parentready.com

Parent Ready and design are trademarks of Parent Ready, Inc.

The publisher is not responsible for websites (or their contents) that are not owned by the publisher.

ISBN: 979-8-9880158-1-9 (paperback)
ISBN: 979-8-9880158-2-6 (e-book)

Bulk purchases: Quantity discounts are available. Please make inquiries via https://collegeready.guide.

Table of Contents

Contributors vii
Preface xvii
Introduction xxi

Chapter 1: What Is the Sophomore Slump? 1
How to prepare for second-year challenges
Stephanie Stiltner

Chapter 2: Is It Too Soon to Step Back? 9
How to coach your student to independence
Lynanne Jamison, Ed.D.

Chapter 3: What if My Student Wants to Change Their Major? 17
How to support your student through new
    academic challenges
Rebecca Downing

Chapter 4: What if My Student Struggles Academically? 25
How to help your student find academic support
Kesha Williams

Chapter 5: Should My Student Study Abroad? 33
Exploring the option to learn in another country
Jenny Sullivan

Chapter 6: When Should My Student Start Building
Their Resume? 43
How to prepare for the job search through
    campus opportunities
Joni O'Hagan and Michelle Kyriakides, Ed.D.

Chapter 7: How Might My Student Change During College? . . . 55
  How to prepare for your student's identity exploration
  Maureen Hurley

Chapter 8: Should I Worry About My Student's Well-Being? 63
  How to encourage self-care and wellness
  Carrie Glatting and Samantha Jeffries, LMFT

Chapter 9: How Will I Know if Something Is Wrong? 73
  How to recognize signs of struggle
  Trish Moser and Penelope Strater

Chapter 10: What Does It Mean To Be a Campus Leader? 83
  How to encourage continued engagement
  Bridget Guernsey Riordan

Chapter 11: How Important Is My Student's Social Circle? 93
  How to support an ever-changing social life
  Whitney White

Chapter 12: How Far Off Campus Is This Apartment? 101
  How to navigate choices about where to live
  Marshall Greenleaf, Ed.D.

Chapter 13: What If Something Goes Wrong? 109
  How to respond to personal or campus-wide emergencies
  Chelsea Petree, Ph.D.

Chapter 14: Is My Student Junior Ready? 115
  How to prepare for next year
  Lindsey Bray

Conclusion 123

This book is dedicated to the parents, families, and caregivers of college sophomores as you guide your student through the next chapter of their college experience.

Contributors

Editor

Chelsea Petree, Ph.D.
Rochester Institute of Technology

Chelsea Petree is the Parent and Family Programs director at Rochester Institute of Technology (RIT). Chelsea moved to Rochester in 2015 to establish the Parent and Family Programs office, including developing a comprehensive parent communications plan and implementing family events and engagement opportunities. She has worked to establish a "parents as partners" culture at RIT, increasing support of families across the institution. Chelsea received her Ph.D. in family social science from the University of Minnesota in 2013 and has served on the Board of Directors and as president of AHEPPP: Family Engagement in Higher Education. She has won several awards, including the 2019 Rising Alumni Award from the College of Education and Human Development at the University of Minnesota and the 2021 AHEPPP Powerful Partnership Award for Tiger Parent Project—a program that brings together RIT staff and faculty to learn more about the family experience and parent-student-university relationships. She is the editor of the College Ready book series.

Contributors

Lindsey Bray
Cornell University

Lindsey Bray serves as the director of Parent and Family Programs at Cornell University. She has worked with parents and families of college students for more than 13 years. Lindsey earned her bachelor's degree in political science from the University of Tennessee, Knoxville; her master's degree in history; and graduate certificates in museum studies and philanthropy and nonprofit leadership from the University of Memphis. She is currently working on her Ed.D. in adult and higher education from the University of Memphis. Before joining Cornell, she launched the University of Memphis Parent and Family Services office and served as the department head for six years. Lindsey serves on the AHEPPP: Family Engagement in Higher Education board of directors.

Rebecca Downing
Colgate University

Rebecca Downing is senior director of communications and parent initiatives at Colgate University, where she has worked since 1996—for many of those years as the alumni magazine editor. Previously, she was an editor/writer at Syracuse University's College of Visual and Performing Arts and Wentworth Institute of Technology, and she also worked in customer service for the educational publisher Course Technology. She earned her BA in creative writing from Hamilton College. Rebecca created Colgate's communications program for family members beginning in 2019; she enjoys advising them and serving as a liaison between campus departments. More than 30 years in higher education have given her insights that make her a resource for families to support their students.

Carrie Glatting
RMHCI, Orlando

Carrie Glatting serves the Central Florida community as a registered mental health counseling intern, guiding clients as they discover meaning to discomfort and distress in their lives. Prior to her role as a counselor, Carrie served as assistant director with the Student and Family Care office at Rollins College, where she provided holistic support to students and families navigating college life. She also served on the parent engagement committee and contributed to the parent and family communications team. Carrie began her career at Rollins as a program counselor, then as director of two Trio Programs, Upward Bound and Educational Talent Search. Carrie has also taught College Success courses for first-generation students.

Marshall Greenleaf, Ed.D.
University of Massachusetts Lowell

Marshall Greenleaf is the director of Student and Family Support Services at the University of Massachusetts Lowell. Marshall has been at UMass Lowell since 2008 and has served in various roles in Residence Life and Family Programs before launching the new Student and Family Support Services office in fall 2021. Marshall's work focuses on three distinct areas: family programs, resources for students experiencing housing and food insecurity, and off-campus living resources. Marshall received his Ed.D. in higher education administration from New England College, and he holds a master's degree from James Madison University and a bachelor's degree from Colby-Sawyer College. Marshall serves on the AHEPPP: Family Engagement in Higher Education board of directors. He is originally from Maine, and currently lives in New Hampshire with his husband, Jim, and mini-schnauzer, Henry.

Maureen Hurley
Emerson College

Maureen Hurley is part of the campus life team at Emerson College in Boston, where she oversees Student Transitions and Family Programs. Maureen has been at Emerson for more than eight years and loves the creative vibe that runs through the community. Prior to her arrival at Emerson, she worked at her alma mater, Boston University (at both the Boston and London campuses), where she earned both an undergraduate and graduate degree. She also worked for the British School of Boston as the director of admissions. Maureen serves on the board of directors of AHEPPP: Family Engagement in Higher Education. In addition to the College Ready series, Maureen has also contributed to *Partnering with the Parents and Family Members of Today's College Students: Innovations in Practice* (2024).

Lynanne Jamison, Ed.D.
Virginia Commonwealth University

Lynanne Jamison is the associate dean for Families and Family Programs at Virginia Commonwealth University and has worked in higher education for 20 years, serving parents and families directly in a professional capacity for more than a decade. She previously served in various positions within residential life, student leadership, and campus activities at Georgia Southern University, Virginia Tech, and the University of Tennessee. Lynanne has presented locally and nationally about best practices in family engagement and has held various leadership roles in numerous professional associations, including AHEPPP. Lynanne completed her Ed.D. in leadership at Virginia Commonwealth University, her MS in college student personnel from the University of Tennessee, and her BA in sociology from Christopher Newport University. She champions student and family advocacy, with a particular passion for building increased support for first-generation families, students in crisis, and post-traditional students with parenting or caregiving responsibilities.

Samantha Jeffries, LMFT
Rochester Institute of Technology

Samantha Jeffries serves as the Associate Director of Student Case Management at Rochester Institute of Technology (RIT). In this role, she helps students, parents, and families navigate resources and support services both on campus and within the Rochester community. She also serves as a member of RIT's Student Behavior Consultation Team, which is tasked with coordinating resources and support for students of concern. In addition to her work at RIT, Samantha serves as a member of the Conference Planning Committee and the Non-Clinical Case Manager Committee within the Higher Education Case Managers Association (HECMA). Samantha's main areas of focus in her work are mental health, crisis navigation, and community education. Prior to joining RIT, Samantha worked in community mental health, as well as within private practice and online telehealth platforms. She is a licensed marriage and family therapist (LMFT) in New York State. She earned her BA in psychology from the University of Rochester, and her MS in marriage and family therapy from the University of Rochester School of Medicine and Dentistry.

Michelle Kyriakides, Ed.D.
Hofstra University

Michelle Kyriakides, executive director of the Center for Career Design and Development at Hofstra University, has 20 years of experience in career counseling, experiential learning, and higher education administration. Prior to working in higher education, she worked in the communications industry, supporting college students from across the country as they interned at national media outlets in New York

City and serving as the manager of public relations for a nonprofit organization. Michelle has taught graduate courses in higher education administration focused on career counseling, student retention, and data management. She has presented locally and nationally about program assessment, data-driven decision making, and her collaborative work with faculty and across campus divisions. Michelle earned an Ed.D. in instructional leadership and an MS.Ed. in student development practices in higher education at St. John's University, an MA in television/film from Syracuse University's S.I. Newhouse School for Public Communications, and a BA in communication and philosophy from the University of Scranton.

Trish Moser
Rollins College

Trish Moser serves as director of the Office of Student Affairs at Rollins College in Winter Park, Florida. Prior to Rollins, Trish served as the director of Alumni and Parent Relations at Loyola University in New Orleans. Trish has 25 years of higher education experience in the areas of institutional advancement and academic and student affairs. She holds a master's degree in mental health counseling. As director of the Office of Student Affairs, she is a member of the student affairs leadership team and is responsible for leadership, project management, and the connection of divisional and institutional priorities. Trish convenes and leads a cross-functional team of campus partners to manage parent and family communication and Family Weekend at Rollins.

Joni O'Hagan
St. John's University

Joni O'Hagan, executive director of the Center for Student Success at St. John's University, has 25 years of experience in higher education within campus activities, leadership development, career services, mentoring, parent and family engagement, and student success. In her current role, she oversees a one-stop hub of resources for first-year students, which includes academic and career advising, academic achievement resources and tutoring, mentoring, and other first-year transition programs. Additionally, she teaches public speaking and business writing as an adjunct professor at St. John's. In addition to her full-time responsibilities, she holds memberships in NACADA, AHEPPP, EACE, NACE and NASPA, and MNYCCPOA. She holds a BA in history from the University of Delaware and an MS in education and an advanced certificate in instructional leadership from St. John's University.

Bridget Guernsey Riordan

Bridget Guernsey Riordan is a higher education consultant focused on student development, program management, and parent and family engagement. She served in student affairs at Emory University for over 30 years prior to her retirement in 2023. Bridget hails from Indiana and received her BS degree from Ball State University. She began her career as a National Collegiate Field Advisor for Alpha Chi Omega. She received her M.Ed. from the University of Cincinnati and Ph.D. from the University of Pittsburgh, and she worked in student affairs positions at both institutions. At Emory, Bridget served as Director of Student Activities, Dean of Students and Assistant Vice President for Campus Life. During her career, Bridget has received several honors including Emory Campus Life's Ethical Leadership Award, Research and Publication Award, and Helen Jenkins Lifetime Achievement Award.

Stephanie Stiltner
University of Pikeville

Stephanie Stiltner is the director of Family and New Student Connections at the University of Pikeville (UPIKE) in Kentucky, a program she had the opportunity to develop in 2018. In her current position, she oversees family engagement and first- and second-year experience programs for undergraduate students. Her previous experience in higher education includes serving in the university's Office of Public Affairs, where she developed a diverse skill set and widespread knowledge about the institution, both of which she puts into use every day as she serves families and students. She holds bachelor's and master's degrees in communication. She is also a contributing author to *College Ready: Expert Advice for Parents to Simplify the College Transition*. Stephanie is the proud mother of Amelia, who is her sidekick and mini-me.

Penelope Strater
Rollins College

Penelope Strater serves as the associate dean of students and director of Student and Family Care at Rollins College in Winter Park, Florida. In 2014, she developed the office of Student and Family Care to provide nonclinical, case management services for students and assist them in navigating their college experience, from matriculation through graduation. She works closely with multidisciplinary partners to manage student crises and concerns and strengthen student retention, persistence, and success. Penelope is a doctoral candidate in the doctor of education, educational leadership, and organizational innovation program at Marymount University. She holds an M.Ed. in educational psychology with a concentration in special education and a BA in educational psychology and child psychology from the University of Minnesota.

Jenny Sullivan
Rochester Institute of Technology

Jenny Sullivan traveled overseas for the first time as an undergraduate to Harlaxton College in England through her school, the University of Evansville. Her love of travel and learning about other cultures inspired her to earn her master's degree in higher education administration from Oregon State University. She has since lived in Ireland and Ecuador and has worked in international education for 15 years. She is currently the director of Education Abroad and International Fellowships at Rochester Institute of Technology in New York.

Whitney White
University of Cincinnati

Whitney White is the director of Parent and Family Programs at the University of Cincinnati. She is passionate about engaging families in the higher education experience and equipping them to be essential partners in their student's success. She founded the inaugural parent and family programs offices at both Johns Hopkins University in 2016 and the University of California–Santa Barbara in 2008. She has higher education experience in orientation programs, academic advising, and learning assistance services. Whitney holds a master of education in academic advising from Kansas State University and is currently pursuing a doctorate of education in urban educational leadership from the University of Cincinnati. She serves on the board of directors for AHEPPP: Family Engagement in Higher Education.

Kesha Williams
Saint Louis University

Kesha Williams serves as the Director for Parent and Family Engagement in the Dean of Students within the division of Student Development at Saint Louis University (SLU). She has worked in higher education for more than 25 years and specifically with parents and families for more than 15 vyears. Before that time, she worked at Johns Hopkins University as the Director for Parent and Family Relations. In her role at SLU, she partners with Enrollment and Recruitment management, Alumni Development, and Student Development on comprehensive strategies on how to engage families. She also develops programming and communication initiatives for the Office of Parent and Family Engagement and serves as the parent liaison to the Billiken Parent and Family Association (BPFA). Kesha has served on the Board of Directors of AHEPPP: Family Engagement in Higher Education.

Preface

Every two years, I conduct a survey of parents and family members at Rochester Institute of Technology (RIT), where I work, to learn more about them. What are their concerns? How are they using RIT family programming? How are they supporting their student throughout their time on campus? Recently, I uncovered the most interesting finding. Across a list of topics (e.g., academics, health, safety, housing, relationships), knowledge of campus resources decreased significantly in their students' sophomore year.

If you think about the path of a college parent, this makes sense. Parents are right next to their student as they begin their college search, tour campuses, and attend orientation. As the parent of a first-year student, you know everything…except what you don't know. Many students do not experience significant challenges in their first year, and by the second year everything students and parents learned about academic support, mental health resources, and involvement opportunities during an admissions event has long left their memories. It makes sense that, as a student enters their second year and begins to encounter new challenges and experiences, parents learn that they don't know as much about support resources as they thought they did one year before or prior.

The concept of the "sophomore slump" is not new. We know that students in their second year of college are often let down, as they don't receive the same fanfare they did the year before, classes get harder, and what they thought were solid friendships start to shift. We know these students can struggle. But what about you—the parents, family members, and supporters of the sophomore? How has your experience changed, and how does your involvement in your student's life shift as you do what you were asked to do since day one—let go and let your student lead?

For many of you, sophomore year is going to be a breeze. Your student is on the right path and can advocate for themselves and move ahead with few challenges. But you also might find your student questioning things they have always been certain of and maybe even asking questions you don't know how to answer. This might be something big, like wanting to change from a premed major to visual arts or questioning the faith they were raised in and exploring other options. It might be something minor, like dying their hair purple or joining the rock-climbing club when they've always expressed a fear of heights. Either way, just as your student faces new challenges as a sophomore, you will find yourself in new territory as a sophomore parent.

The goal of this book is to help you navigate your student's sophomore year, with all the challenges and the joys it will bring. Even though you may have to talk your student through stressful situations, you will get to watch them navigate life, discover new passions, and develop into the adult they will be.

I am lucky to have the opportunity to work with so many amazing people as the College Ready series grows. I am grateful for my publisher, Parent Ready, who cares so much about the parent experience that this series will soon stretch across the high school and college years. A huge thank you to our copy editor for her editing skills and to Anja Schmidt for keeping me on track. I greatly admire the contributors of this book for their dedication to the field and willingness to work outside their own campuses by sharing their vast knowledge within these pages to help support all parents. A special shout-out to M, W, and L, who jumped in to support me in the final hour.

I will forever be grateful to AHEPPP: Family Engagement in Higher Education and the life-changing opportunities it has brought to my life and how its members positively impact the lives of college parents daily.

To the parents, family members, and supporters of college students: I love my job every day because of you. Your passion and care for your students shines through in every encounter. I'm excited to be a part of this next chapter of your journey.

Chelsea Petree, Ph.D.
College Sophomore Ready **Editor**
Director, Parent & Family Programs
Rochester Institute of Technology

Introduction

This book is for the parents, family members, and supporters who are finding themselves in new territory as their college student enters their sophomore year.

You think you made it. You got them off to college last year, and that was supposed to be the hard part, right? It should be smooth sailing until graduation. But what about that call sometime during your student's second year, where you hear, "I don't like engineering anymore—I'm going to change my major to English," "Guess what—I'm going to Morocco!", "I've been struggling getting out of bed in the morning," or "I know you didn't want me to, but I got a tattoo." Suddenly, you realize you aren't the college parent expert you thought you were, even after you made it through move-in day last year with no tears (at least until you got to the car).

Sophomore year is brand-new territory for many students. Classes get harder, expectations increase, and students begin making decisions that will impact their entire lives. The whole "adulting" thing starts to get real. Moreover, sophomore year is *different*. Campus and college life aren't new and exciting anymore. Friends are no longer next door or down the hall. Sophomores are neither the new kids on campus nor are they the experienced seniors. They are somewhere in the middle, trying to figure out who they are on campus and in life.

It is not uncommon for students in their second year to start questioning things they thought they were very sure about. They may start to rethink their majors and career goals as they take electives that are interesting to them. They will continue to be exposed to new identities, cultures, and belief systems through study abroad, club activities, and new friends from around the world. They may come home a vegan, or a Buddhist, or sporting an interesting piercing or hairstyle....

While the idea of these changes and challenges might make you nervous, there is excitement to be found in what lies ahead. The harder classes mean your student is learning more and becoming passionate about their field of study. The opportunity to study abroad offers a chance to return home with a new world view. Not having friends next door means they will again have to get out of their comfort zone to meet new people, and they will learn the value of true friendship. The opportunity for growth is endless this year, as are the possibilities for your student.

As you will read in this book, you can expect more phone calls or texts from your student this year with questions and worries. Some may seem big at the time, but remember to stay calm and encourage your student to consider their passions, strengths, and campus resources while working through challenges. Your role continues to be important as you support your student through the new, the exciting, and the scary.

The chapters ahead cover many aspects of the sophomore year and are written by professionals in the areas of family engagement, mental health, study abroad, career services, and the second-year experience. The content will help you help your student navigate this year with information, resources, and conversation starters.

Not all college students have the same path. What some students experience their first year, others will not encounter until their third. So, while the content of this book covers issues typical of the second year in college, your student may have already experienced some of these things or may not encounter them at all. Every family is different, and parts of the book will resonate differently with each reader. Parents have their own experiences to contribute, and this book will provide perspective and guidance no matter your knowledge on each topic.

Welcome to the next chapter of your college journey!

Chapter 1
WHAT IS THE SOPHOMORE SLUMP?

How to prepare for second-year challenges

Stephanie Stiltner
University of Pikeville

Your student's senior year of high school was full of memorable lasts—last formal dances, last athletic events, and last traditions. Their first year of college was marked by a series of firsts—first time away from home, first roommate, and first taste of true freedom. The two years leading up to your student's second year of college have been filled with countless celebrations and milestones, along with a roller coaster of emotions.

Think of the first year of college as bowling with the bumpers up. Students have a clearly defined path and can see the goal straight ahead, with a team of people lined up along the gutters to help keep them on track. Of course, student support doesn't end after their first year on campus, but the second year comes with its own unique challenges.

Why is the Sophomore Year Different?

When students begin their second year of college, there is little to no fanfare, as welcome weeks and move-in receptions typically are hosted for first-year students. For some students, it may feel as if the "new" has worn off. Preparing to move back to campus and loading up your vehicle with the same dorm essentials from last year that have been crammed into your bedroom at home just does not provide the same level of excitement as cutting the tags off the new towels or unboxing your new single-cup coffee maker.

As your student settles into their second year in college, they may begin thinking, "Is this it? Is this what the rest of my college career is going to be like?" The things that just a year ago gave them wonder now have become routine. Learning to do laundry with your new roommate and laughing about shrinking your favorite sweater turns into waiting to do laundry until you have no clean socks.

The sophomore year can feel like being the middle child. No longer the newest student on campus, nor an upperclassman, you're somewhere in the middle, trying to figure out what's next. Students who haven't connected with the campus community or settled on a major may wonder if they are doing the right thing, and impostor syndrome may set in.

Second-year students can feel as if they are expected to know everything about the ins and outs of campus because they are no longer first-year students. That pressure may cause them to hesitate to reach out for help, but it's important to encourage them to seek out resources available to them. Supporting your student during this phase may be as simple as reassuring them that this is part of the process. Normalizing their experiences is sometimes all they need to know that they are on the right path.

Shifting Friendships

During your student's first year on campus, they likely formed connections with other new students. Those relationships were important and helped your student navigate their first year. Some relationships will continue past the first year, while your student may realize they have outgrown others. Let your student know that it is okay and part of growing and maturing.

Students may choose to live with a new roommate or hang out with a different friend group. Friendships often form as students begin spending more time with classmates who share the same interests. As your student digs deeper into their major, they may realize they are surrounded by people who get them. When we are young, friendship is often based on proximity, like living in the same neighborhood or having a homeroom together all through middle school. College friendships are different. College provides an opportunity for students from all across the world to come together because of shared chosen interests. The bonds made between college friends are strong and may last a lifetime.

A surefire way for students to be successful throughout college is to be engaged on campus. Involvement in clubs, honor societies, and athletics may come to mind first, but there are countless ways to be involved. As your student progresses in college, more and more opportunities become available. Refer to Chapter 10 for information on how to encourage your student to be involved.

Crucial Connections

Students may also start to form meaningful connections with faculty. It's common for students to have the same professor for multiple classes within their major. Spending more time together in the classroom and during office hours can help students get to know their professors. These relationships are important, because professors can mentor, write letters of recommendation for graduate school, or serve as a resume reference. Students often build similar relationships with staff in support services departments, including the tutoring or career centers.

During the first year of college, students typically take classes that fulfill general education requirements. Classes are often comprised of first-year students who are going through the same experiences. Students who haven't selected a major may continue to take general education courses their second year, while students who have chosen a major will likely be taking upper-level courses within their major. Content is harder and the amount of studying increases; this may be the first time your student struggles academically. Now is a good time to remind them that time management is their responsibility. Prioritizing time to study and complete assignments is a necessity and may help them mitigate stress.

Major Decisions

Stressors for second-year students are different from the ones they experienced during their first year, and many of those stressors are centered around finding their passion in a major they love. At many universities, students are encouraged to explore majors during their first year to learn about fields they may be interested in, and then they suddenly feel pressured to choose a major their second year. Even though their first year was designed to help them select a major, they may feel as if this decision is sudden and scary. Keep in mind that when students don't know the path they are taking, or don't yet fully understand the value of higher education, they may be more likely to make academic decisions that will lead to poor grades, extended time until graduation, or questions about what to do after college.

Some students are sure of their major and career choice, but many are not. Even if they feel as if they know what they want to be when they grow up, they can still struggle with issues relating to their major. Students may come to college passionate about pursuing a specific major, but when they start taking the harder classes, self-doubt sets in. Some choose a major based on what they think they might like, but when the course material doesn't match their interests or what they enjoy, they question their decision. Others may have a hard time letting go of what was once their ideal career because they have wanted to be a teacher, doctor, video game designer—insert childhood dream here—since they were in grade school. No matter what goes into a student's decision-making as they choose a major, know that it's a big deal. You'll find more information about supporting your student through academic challenges as you continue reading this book.

Let's not forget that family can be influential during this process. Some students worry that they will let their family down, while others feel pressure to pursue a degree that will lead to a particular career. The best advice for families is to support your student's decision on a major and to keep their true passions and interests in mind, rather than what you may *think* they would be good at. Students who are happy with their major will be more successful, and you can best support this path by coaching your student to independence.

In addition to choosing a major, second-year students are often encouraged to participate in campus programming centered around career development, leadership, and networking. They may be asked to consider job shadowing or selecting an internship. This may cause added stress, because it again has students thinking about their post-college plans.

Different Paths During the Second Year

Before your student started college, you may have worried about the adjustment to certain aspects of college life, only to breathe a sigh of relief when those issues didn't arise. Don't be caught off guard if those concerns resurface during your student's second year. Some students are hesitant to explore their freedom during their first year and delay certain college life experiences until their second year.

Students who did well during their first year may return to campus for their second year with an "I've got this" attitude. This mindset, along with taking harder courses, can be a risky combination. Choosing to stay up late to play video games can lead to oversleeping and missing an early class. Underestimating the time needed for studying, finishing a project, or researching for a paper can lead to their first bad grade on a test. These things happening occasionally is part of being a college student and should be viewed as a learning experience, but these behaviors can quickly turn into habits that have high costs.

Some students experience tremendous growth their first year. For others, that happens during their second year. On the other hand, students who struggled their first year often find their way and settle in during their second year. Students are quick to turn things around when they realize their academic and social actions (or inactions) are important.

Closing Advice

Whether your student completed their first year with few challenges or took a little extra time to adjust to college and all the new experiences that come with it, know that they are where they need to be in their collegiate journey. Don't get stuck on the idea of the right or wrong way your student should experience college. This is their journey. Their path through each year of college will be different. Give them the confidence to know you will be there along the way.

> **Conversation Starters**
>
> - How do you think your second year on campus will be different from the first?
> - What are you most looking forward to about your second year?
> - Tell me about your new roommates.
> - How does it feel to not be one of the "new kids" on campus?
> - Are you satisfied with your major?
> - What clubs and organizations are you interested in?
> - Is there anything you feel hesitant about as you go into your second year?
> - How are the activities and programs on campus feeding your passions and interests?

Conversation Starters

Chapter 2

IS IT TOO SOON TO STEP BACK?

How to coach your student to independence

Lynanne Jamison, Ed.D.
Virginia Commonwealth University

Last year, you may have been told your student is now an adult and you need to let go. You may have been encouraged to let your student make their own decisions and mistakes. Maybe you did. Maybe not. Every student's path is unique, and their approach to navigating college and life as a young adult is no different. Similarly, every family member experiences a distinct journey supporting their student through everything this season of life offers (or sometimes throws at) them.

Sophomore year is filled with decisions to make. Many campuses require students to declare a major this year. Some do not provide on-campus housing after the first year, so students must determine where and with whom they will live. It's a time for getting more involved in student organizations and exploring the idea of becoming a campus leader. Some students may contemplate getting their first internship, job, or even (yikes!) leaving the country to study abroad. Take a breath. It's a lot...but your student can handle it, and so can you. With the advice found in this book, you'll be coaching your student to become more independent before another semester passes.

The Difference Between Giving Advice and Giving Answers

How often have you shared something with a loved one, friend, or colleague, only for them to begin the next sentence with, "You should... [insert something that sounds like a solution here]"? It is natural for humans to listen while simultaneously formulating a response that will be perceived as supportive. It's even more natural to do this for your child. After all, it has been your responsibility to teach them how to respond and provide answers to their questions. It's possible they may have needed this from you during their first year in college. The need for support doesn't ever go away, but your approach should shift so you are teaching your student how to strategize solutions that work for them.

As your student progresses through sophomore year, they may choose to share more information with you. It may be more than you thought they would share or maybe even more than you wanted to hear! Understand that there are times they aren't looking for you to respond with a course of action to take. They may just want to get concerns off their chest. It's okay (and encouraged) to respond by asking if they would like your advice before giving it.

If they agree to receive advice, phrase it as such and not as an answer. The difference between giving an answer and providing advice is simple: An answer does not encourage more conversation, sometimes makes assumptions or inserts opinions, and always ends with a period. Advice acknowledges what was said and might contain options or personal experiences. It may end with a question to keep the conversation going.

Let's take a look at how a few phrases you might use with your sophomore could be framed as advice instead of answers. You get bonus points if you can end your advice with an action that encourages developing independence.

ANSWER	ADVICE
You should get that mole checked out by a doctor.	I'm concerned about you. Have you seen a doctor? I can give you my dermatologist's number if you want to make an appointment.
I would demand a raise if I were you.	It seems like you should be eligible for a promotion or extra help at work. If you ever want to practice asking for that, I'm here.
You should go on a date with this person.	You seem to be really connecting with this person. Do you want to see them again?
I know you really don't want to change your major again.	I want you to be happy. You also have to think about extending your degree timeline. Have you weighed the pros and cons of another major change? Sometimes it helps to make a list.
I would give them a piece of my mind!	I had a friend like that once and things got better when I told them how I felt. Does your roommate know how you feel?
You should not buy that outfit for your interview.	You look great. Have you observed what other people wear at this office? Is it appropriate for your job interview?
I think you should study abroad in Scotland.	I wish I'd studied abroad! I really wanted to go to Scotland. What are some of the countries you're excited about?

By changing how you phrase your response, you show you are listening and offering support. You may even offer information that leads them down a solid path without making decisions on their behalf. This is one of the many ways to begin coaching your student to independence.

Take a Step Back

Anytime we accomplish something in life, it's wise to take a step back and evaluate how we did. Encourage your student to reflect on their first year and do some goal-setting related to the big decisions they will make during their second year. Conduct a self-analysis of your involvement in their transition to college. Don't be afraid to set a few goals for removing yourself a little more from their decision-making processes going into this new year. Consider, for example:

- When was my involvement/input helpful to my student? How was it helpful?
- When was my involvement/input not helpful? What might I have done differently?
- What big decisions will my student make this year, and how can I be supportive?
- What expectations do I have about involvement in their decisions? Are these realistic?

Stepping back metaphorically will help you prepare to step back physically so your student can begin making more independent choices and identifying when they need your guidance. You can still give advice and be a source of emotional support. Allow your student to come to you for guidance rather than inserting yourself or saving the day. There may be opportunities for you to intervene. Ask yourself if the consequence is truly worth preventing. Stepping back gives your student autonomy and teaches them to seek help and course correct when they make mistakes.

Leaning In

If you just got nervous reading the words "course correct," it's okay. You are not alone. Many families struggle with this. Some mistakes are big, with big consequences. Stepping back does not mean stepping away. You're allowed (encouraged!) to lean in. But leaning in requires that you have first stepped back and given your student space to make mistakes and decisions independently. From this new vantage point, you may see your student in an entirely different light.

There are a few key techniques to effectively lean in and help as needed:

Listen to All Language

Listen when your student speaks, and pay attention to their body language and what it's saying about how things are going. If you don't see your student regularly, suggest video chatting so you don't miss their facial expressions and gestures. Our bodies speak more than our mouths.

Offer Advice…And Ask for It, Too

See the section on page 11 on how to give advice instead of providing answers. Then, show your student you respect their decision-making by asking them for advice about something you are currently dealing with.

Read Up on Resources

There's a good chance that while your sophomore is practicing independence, they will procrastinate when asking for help. Get ahead of this by being up-to-date on campus resources. Explore websites (especially ones related to their academic program and student support services), read newsletters for families so you know all the tips and tricks, and stay abreast of upcoming opportunities and deadlines via social media. This will also give you things to suggest they explore.

Know Their "Person," and Find Yours

Your student should have a designated person on campus to help them navigate challenges. It is likely an academic advisor, a peer mentor, or a faculty member. Know who that person is and ask if they've talked to that person when they bring up questions or concerns. Identify someone, like a family programs professional, whom you can call for help when you need additional information or advice.

Be Vulnerable

Your student will make mistakes. Let your guard down, and don't be afraid to share the mistakes you've made in the past. This will lead to a more honest and open relationship with them now and in the future.

Offer Comfort…But Not Too Much of the Comforts of Home

Sometimes sophomores who have a difficult time connecting to campus life return home frequently. Encourage them to join a student organization, play a club sport, or get a job near campus.

Celebrate!

When you lean in effectively, you become aware not just of things that aren't going well, but also of things that are going very well. When your student accomplishes something independently or achieves a goal, celebrate in whatever way works for your family—a verbal acknowledgement, a text saying you're proud of them, a care package, or the treat of a dinner out.

You know your student better than just about anyone. You know their strengths and challenges and can adjust how much you lean in accordingly. There are many factors that determine how much you should lean in. Factors like neurodivergence and/or disability status, health conditions, and personality traits all play a part in determining how much coaching your student may need to become more independent.

Letting GrOw

During their first year in college, there were so many people on campus keeping a close eye on your student and providing support and advice. If they lived on campus, their resident advisor (RA) was popping in to say hello. Their academic advisor was reaching out to make sure things were going well. Other first-year students were trying to make friends, so they felt commonality and, hopefully, community. In the second year, the resources on campus are still in place, but your student has to initiate conversations and seek assistance.

Encouraging your student to develop these skills now will absolutely pay off. This is hard. It's so easy to step in instead of lean in. You've been there and done that, and you know all the answers, right? Remind yourself that you are not letting them go—you are letting them *grow*. Part of that process must include developing resilience through:

- Managing their feelings
- Problem-solving independently and discovering when help is needed
- Communicating effectively
- Understanding how to prioritize their well-being
- Building confidence and realizing self-worth
- Being able to set and achieve realistic goals

Closing Advice

Allow your student to work on these skills with as much independence as possible. When you see these things happening, celebrate them. Remember: That's part of leaning in. And if it's not happening at the pace you expected, try not to sweat it. Your student will get there.

> ### Conversation Starters
>
> - Is there anything you are nervous or excited about this year that you'd like my advice or feedback on?
> - How did I do with offering you support during your first year? Is there more (or less) you need from me as you start a new year?
> - Who is "your person" on campus? How often are you checking in with them?
> - How do you practice self-care? In what ways do you make yourself a priority?
> - What goals have you set for yourself this year? How can I support you?

Chapter 3

WHAT IF MY STUDENT WANTS TO CHANGE THEIR MAJOR?

How to support your student through new academic challenges

Rebecca Downing
Colgate University

After two semesters of introductory classes and the extra advising support given to first-year students, sophomores experience more challenging coursework and new academic pressures. They have gained (we hope) a sense of what subjects excite them and the expectations of college professors. Now they need to become more introspective about what they are studying and how it relates to their degree and career goals. Yet there are still new academic skills to learn and build upon. You might hear that it all just feels harder. They don't have it all down yet!

Understanding the driving forces of your sophomore's academic journey will help you support them as they progress toward their degree. This chapter shares insights that can help if your student brings up their major in conversation.

How to Think About the Major

Academic challenges that sophomores may face include deciding upon a major, developing a solid plan for their coursework, and falling off track as a result of the "sophomore slump" you read about in Chapter 1. But they are not alone! Colleges and universities employ staff and faculty to support students as they make decisions or when they run into a snag. These resources include academic advisors, department or program chairs, professors teaching courses of interest, and career services staff. At some schools, students also have a non-faculty advising administrator or administrative dean who can provide guidance on their college plan.

The Importance of Interest and Motivation

When we are interested in something (e.g., a hobby, friendship, civic involvement), we are more likely to feel invested and dedicate time to it. We are fueled by intrinsic motivation. The same is true for a major.

The major is a requirement for a degree for which students will take a deep dive into a specific area of study. Some majors, such as engineering, provide particular knowledge and experience for that career area. Even students pursuing a liberal arts degree, which typically has a wider range of requirements, have the opportunity to fully immerse themselves in a subject through their major. The material may not directly relate to an eventual career path, but as they learn, they will be developing core skills and intellectual perspectives that will make them successful. In either case, psychologists have found that students learn best when they are intrinsically motivated by the subject. This underscores the importance of selecting a major that is enjoyable, challenging, and satisfying.

Students also feel intrinsically motivated when they are supported by their self-determination. This happens when their needs are fulfilled in three areas:

- **Autonomy.** Students need a sense of freedom and ownership over their academic choices. Support your student's interests as they emerge, and try to avoid making suggestions that they may perceive as directives.
- **Competence.** Students need to feel that they can master the material in their major. Recognizing your student's accomplishments and encouraging them to find support on campus if they are struggling in a course of interest are two ways to support them.
- **Relatedness.** Students experience motivation when they make connections with professors and the other students in their major. Asking your student about the people they are learning from and with can help them recognize those connections. Look for ways to bond around your student's intellectual interests, such as attending department events if you visit campus.

Some students worry that they need to pick a major that employers will value. But all majors produce employable graduates because the value of a college education is about much more than just the major. Internship providers and employers want candidates with curiosity and skills in communication, critical thinking, time management, technology, collaboration, working across differences, and receiving and delivering constructive feedback. Your student will be building these skills, no matter their major. Their major dovetails with other academic courses, extracurricular activities, internships, research, career services programs, and leadership opportunities. For instance, a premed major can volunteer on the local ambulance corps. College is comprehensive preparation.

Deciding Upon and Declaring a Major

Declaring a major is an important moment. Students should have a sense of how specific their postgraduate goals are so they can be sure to choose a program that will meet them. For example, the major can be a factor in graduate school admission.

Shaping Their Decision

Some students may be certain about their course of study. Others might wrestle with the choice and need support in thinking through their decision. It's helpful to look beyond their grades thus far to see areas where they are most motivated to learn. If your student isn't sure about their academic choices, career direction, or how to shape their path, encourage them to tap the resources and services available to them. Strategies for their process might include:

- Carefully reading course descriptions and requirements for majors (and minors) of interest
- Talking with juniors and seniors in the major about their experiences, likes, and dislikes
- Making an appointment with the career services office to explore how different majors fit with their goals
- Meeting with the department chair and professors teaching courses in the major
- Attending events hosted by the department, which are great opportunities to meet faculty members and current majors and get a feel for the experience
- Meeting with their advisor(s) to synthesize their research and thoughts

Occasionally, students will pursue two majors (a double major) in subjects that they may consider complementary, such as education and English literature, or that fulfill unrelated interests, such as neuropsychology and art history. Some students also choose one or more minors in a secondary subject that may or may not be related to the major.

Students should prepare for meetings or discussions with professors and advisors in order to receive the best guidance. They can reflect upon their areas of curiosity (academic, professional, extracurricular), the types of classes or activities they have (or haven't) enjoyed so far and why, and aspects of their personal identity that they bring into their choices.

While, for some students, decision-making comes easily, it may be an acquired skill for others. Encourage your student to reflect on what helped them to sort through decisions in the past. Tell them about a decision you had to make and how you approached it. Did you find any special tools or techniques useful? Sharing your own experience can remind your student that decision-making is a process.

The more your student can bring all aspects of their experience into the discussion, the more their advisors will be able to help them identify pathways, resources, and support that will match their interests, needs, and ambitions and move them toward their goals. This takes time, so starting early is important. The decision can feel complicated, so remind them that pursuing a subject or subjects they find intellectually interesting and enjoyable should be a primary goal.

International students may have special considerations if they would like to stay in the United States for postgraduate internships or work. Their major must fit within the career field in which they would like to work; the U.S. visa process is strict about this. These students should take advantage of the support provided by their school's international student services staff and career services office to ensure that their plan meets the necessary requirements.

The Process of Declaring a Major

When the time comes to declare a major, the school will have a designated process and will provide information about the resources available to help students. The timing varies from school to school, but most require students to declare by the end of sophomore year. At some schools, students must apply to a specific major. Other schools may limit the number of students in a particular major. Students should also be aware of prerequisite courses (the foundational classes that must be passed before being admitted into higher-level courses) they will need to progress through to get to a chosen major. It's important for your student to be familiar with any requirements or stipulations, too.

A meeting with a current academic advisor is a common requirement of the process. Once they declare their major, students will usually be assigned an advisor or will choose one. When students have the opportunity to choose, especially if they want a particular person to advise them, they should ask as early as possible. Faculty advising can be essential to a student's success and satisfaction, so developing a good relationship with the advisor is key. Asking a potential academic advisor face-to-face is a great start. Advising is also most effective when students take responsibility for reading the school's catalog and student handbook and when they seek their advisor's assistance early and often.

Changing Majors

Given the course requirements for a major and overall degree program, students should choose their courses thoughtfully. But sometimes students realize that their major no longer fulfills their interests or, through elective courses, discover strong new interests that make them want to pivot from their original intent. Maybe a new experience or new understanding about their identity has shifted their goals. This might come as a surprise to you ("But you have always wanted to be a doctor!"). Responding with supportive feedback and guidance will help your student navigate the change.

Know that, within reason and within specific time frames, it is usually possible for students to change their major without being too concerned about negative consequences. It can be difficult to get into certain courses, however, especially prerequisites that may not be offered every year, which might delay graduation. Students who wish to change their major should review the school's process and requirements and consult with their academic advisor as soon as possible. Career services advisors can also help a student explore how a new major would align with career interests.

If your student is thinking of changing their major, it will be helpful for them to articulate their reasons for the change. Ask questions like:

- What excites you about this new major?
- How would it make a better fit for you?
- What does your advisor say?
- Have you met with any faculty members in that department?
- How are you exploring the new major?
- What differences do you anticipate compared to your current major?
- How will changing your major impact progress in completing your degree?

Pivoting from an intended major might seem worrisome, but it could open up exciting new paths and possibilities for your student's future. The important part is helping them ensure that they have done their homework in thinking through the change.

Closing Advice

Choosing—or changing—a major can feel monumental. If your student asks for assistance, try to avoid undue influence. You can help by asking open-ended questions. Encourage self-reflection and active exploration so that they can be confident in their decision. Help them refocus when they lose track of their goals. Recognizing the opportunities a major provides while keeping perspective on its role in their college education will help you support your student as they make this important choice.

> ### Conversation Starters
>
> - Tell me about the courses you've gotten most excited about. Were there any you did not enjoy? Why?
> - What's been your process in choosing a major? Who on campus are you talking to?
> - Have you attended any events offered by the program you are interested in?
> - What aspects of your personality and identity might be helpful in making your decision?
> - How can you build a plan to make your decision?

Chapter 4
WHAT IF MY STUDENT STRUGGLES ACADEMICALLY?

How to help your student find academic support

Kesha Williams
Saint Louis University

As your student experienced their freshman year, they were able to explore their academic and social interests while building a sense of identity and community. As they prepare for their second year, they may start to feel the impact of decisions they made during their first year. As schedules get busier and coursework becomes more demanding, effective time management and study skills become more essential.

Time Management

Time management is a key component of academic persistence. If your student becomes overwhelmed with a busier schedule and harder classes and starts to notice an impact on their academic performance, consider the role time management is playing. Time management requires organization. Your student should plan on at least two hours of study time per class. This will require commitment to carve out the proper amount of time for class, homework, and studying. Students often believe that they have more time in college because they no longer have a structured eight-hour day in school. Yet they often have not mastered the skill of designing a daily schedule that includes the amount of work required outside of class, as well as activities, social lives, and practical tasks (e.g., cooking and laundry).

If your student is struggling to manage their time, suggest they create a calendar, either electronically or on paper, that includes classes, extracurricular activities, jobs, and time for self-care (e.g., working out, tending to hobbies, socializing). Establishing a comprehensive calendar allows them to see how much time they are dedicating to each activity and to make adjustments as needed. This will also help them avoid missing an assignment, a meeting with their advisor, or a club event. Blocking time for studying before an exam at the beginning of the semester can help remind them to make time for these things and to start preparing earlier than the night before.

To-do lists can also help students stay on track and not get distracted. Daily, weekly, or course-specific to-do lists will keep them focused on their goals and provide reminders of what is ahead. Additionally, the feeling of crossing a task off the list is motivating! Your student's phone or computer hosts many free electronic software platforms that they can use to input and prioritize all their activities and obligations, as well as indicate when they have accomplished their goals.

Study Skills

Students should not underestimate the importance of effective study skills. This looks different for all students and can include keeping up on the reading each week, finding a place on campus with fewer distractions, taking good notes during and outside of class, and applying lessons learned in class to homework assignments. Your student may not recognize that they do not know how to study, they just know that classes are harder than in high school. Understanding and articulating the issue is a necessary first step toward gaining the study skills needed in college. You can help them by asking questions about how and where they study, what skills work well for them, and why they think they are struggling in a particular class.

Most colleges have resources to help students acquire study skills. These offices teach and offer workshops that will show them how to formulate those skills. They also offer tutoring services, seminars, and supplemental instruction dedicated to a class or major, where students can study together. These services will also work with students to identify how they have prepared for a class. This goes beyond the instruction but ensures that students have all the materials they need.

Resources

If your student is struggling with an academic challenge, ask if they are aware of the resources on campus. There are plenty of departments, programs, and people dedicated to supporting students.

Academic Advising

Your student is assigned (or has chosen) an academic advisor who should be one of their primary points of contact. Advisors have been trained in the curriculum and instruction of the college and major, and therefore have the expertise to assist and support your student in designing their academic blueprint to fulfill their graduation requirements. The advisor and student should build trust and rapport with each other; this will help the advisor provide specific suggestions and help your student trust their recommendations.

Prior to advising appointments, students should prepare by writing down a list of questions, concerns, or challenges that they may be facing, like:

- How do students usually determine what they want to major in?
- How long will it take to obtain my degree? Am I on track?
- What is the process for withdrawal from a class? And how does withdrawing affect my academic, financial, and graduation plans?
- When should I investigate internships and take advantage of the office of career services?
- Where can I find tutoring and study skills support services on campus?

Faculty

It is also important that students build a relationship with their professors. Entry-level lecture classes can be very large, making it difficult for a student to stand out or for an instructor to know everyone. If a student is interested in a particular course, professor, or subject area but is finding it difficult to talk to the professor before or after class, they should attend the instructor's office hours. Teaching faculty are required to hold office hours and they will be listed on the course syllabus that is handed out (or provided electronically) on the first day of class. Office hours are designated times that the professor is available for students to pop in for questions or conversation. Many students feel intimidated by the idea of going to office hours at first, but professors welcome the opportunity to talk with students about their questions, achievements, and goals. An office hours visit also indicates to the professor that the student cares about their grade and is committed to their education. If your student is unable to go during the professor's designated hours, they should email the professor to find an alternative meeting time.

Just as they do for advising meetings, students should go to office hours prepared by outlining exactly what they are struggling with and bringing samples of their work. Asking specific questions about why they received certain grades can help them understand what the professor is looking for in assignments and help them improve in the future.

Building relationships with faculty members has benefits beyond getting good grades in a class. Professors make excellent references down the road and may have opportunities to offer in the form of research, teaching assistantships, or office jobs. A simple visit to office hours can open many opportunities for your student.

Here are a few tips to help students have a successful meeting with their professors:

- Remember that you are one of many students in the professor's courses. Remind the professor about the class and section you are in when visiting or sending an email, and introduce yourself with your first and last name.
- Address the professor by the appropriate title and err on the side of formality (e.g., Dr. [last name] or Professor [last name]). They will let you know if they prefer to be called something else by their students.
- Don't be afraid to be personal—tell the professor what clubs or activities you enjoy on campus. Share what you like about their class and what your career goals are. Ask them if they have any advice for you.

Other Academic Staff

If your student is not receiving responses from their academic advisor or a professor or is looking for additional support, there are other staff who love to meet and assist students. A program director oversees each major and will be able to answer questions about coursework and requirements. The college dean has academic, programmatic, and supervisory responsibility for their college. While it is best to start with advisors and professors—and to give them a few days to respond—these and other college staff will also be able to answer questions and offer guidance.

Disability Services

If your student did not have an IEP in high school or use services previously, they might not think about the disability services office as a resource. However, new challenges might be related to an unknown or undiagnosed disability. If your student is finding it difficult to keep up and concentrate, they may need more time for their work. Disability services offices will help identify if your student needs extra support, such as additional time for tests, note-taking assistance, or assignment extensions.

Closing Advice

While there is time to make adjustments later on if needed, sophomore year is when students need to make decisions about their future by choosing their major. This can be intimidating, and students may face new challenges even after one year under their belt. Establishing good academic habits is essential as students confirm their goals for the rest of their college career. Parents are a big part of this process, as you help your student understand the heart of challenges they encounter and point them toward resources.

Conversation Starters

- How have your classes changed this year? Are they harder? More interesting?
- Have you visited your professor's office hours? What did you talk about?
- How do you keep track of your assignments and exams? Do you block time for studying?
- How do you make sure you have time for self-care?
- Are you still on track to graduate on time?

Chapter 5
SHOULD MY STUDENT STUDY ABROAD?

Exploring the option to learn
in another country

Jenny Sullivan
Rochester Institute of Technology

Now that your student has spent a year settling into the college community, they may feel ready for more challenge, independence, and exploration through study abroad. Studies show that study abroad can have significant academic, professional, and personal benefits. Students who participate commonly graduate with higher GPAs, get into their first- or second-choice graduate school, and earn higher salaries. Participants also report that their overseas studies helped them gain key job skills, such as flexibility and problem-solving, and increased their self-confidence. Like interning at a job, conducting undergraduate research, or participating in service learning, studying abroad will yield a good return on investment. Through study abroad, your student can explore their discipline from new perspectives, learn how to adapt and work in diverse settings, develop lifelong relationships, and better understand their role as a member of the global community. In this chapter, we will break down the perceived barriers to study abroad and arm you with the tools to help your student identify when to go and what programs might be the best fit.

Perceived Barriers

There are a few common fears and misperceptions of study abroad, including cost, safety, and academic requirements.

Cost

Often, students assume study abroad is too expensive, when in reality, many programs may be equal or less in cost than the equivalent credits earned at your student's home university. On study abroad, a student should expect to pay tuition (home university tuition or a custom amount); a program fee that will include things like room/board, visa fees, and required cultural excursions; and out-of-pocket expenses such as local transportation and flights. These costs should be clearly outlined by the home university or the study abroad program provider. Many universities allow students to use their regular federal and/or institutional financial aid toward their study abroad program. In addition, your student can apply for scholarships to fund their experience. Study abroad advisors are a great resource for helping students find affordable programs and maximize their budgets by, for example, highlighting programs in regions with a lower cost of living or ones that are significantly subsidized. It is important that your student read and understand the withdrawal, cancellation, and refund guidelines of their preferred programs.

Safety

Another key concern for students and families is safety, and rightfully so. Universities are constantly monitoring their programs around the world, because situations like natural disasters or political protests can affect a student's experience. Because of this, study abroad is dynamic and a program that is available one year might not be available the next. All programs go through rigorous health and safety assessments by the risk management, legal, and study abroad teams at your student's home university. These assessments often include speaking to staff and faculty from other universities and site visits and inspections. If the overseas partner is deemed a good match, the two parties will formalize their relationship in contractual agreements. Universities also develop detailed emergency and communication plans. Faculty and university teams do extensive annual training and update the emergency plans regularly. Students are usually provided with insurance, or instructed how to purchase it, and are required to participate in a lengthy pre-departure program that covers health and safety guidelines, as well as a more location-tailored orientation once they arrive in the country. As with any new environment, students should exercise increased caution, remain aware of their surroundings, and make good choices.

Academic Requirements

Many students think study abroad won't fit into their major or that they can't participate in an experience and still graduate on time. It is true that it may be more challenging to study abroad if they are in a highly specialized discipline, are required to take extensive sequential coursework, come into college with a lot of AP or other college credits, or have other program requirements like research or internships. These students might need to think creatively. For example, they could participate in a zero-credit, international service-learning experience. If their degree program requires an internship, they could do it abroad. Most students can fit in a short-term experience. If your student is set on a semester-long and culturally immersive program, it will be important to plan early. Saving introductory courses, general education requirements, elective credits, and minor courses for a study abroad experience will give your student more flexibility to choose when and where they go.

Assumptions about language often prevent students from exploring the option to study abroad. Many students believe that they must already know a foreign language or are required to study one when they travel. While learning some of the language prior to travel or while in-country can help students settle in, ease culture shock, and gain a deeper understanding of a new place, it's not always required to participate. A study abroad advisor can help your student identify a program that meets their language goals and needs.

These perceived barriers will often prevent a family from considering studying abroad. It's important to avoid assumptions and gather information before discounting the option. You can encourage your student to talk to other students in their major who have already studied abroad, or help them think about questions to ask as they meet with advisors.

Personal Considerations

Cost, location, and length of time are usually the first things students and parents think about when considering a study abroad opportunity, but there are other elements that can make or break an experience. Before they even begin to look for programs, your student should think about what they want to gain from the experience. Is their goal to become fluent in a language? Are they hoping to step out of their comfort zone and become more independent? Are they exploring a location as a potential future destination for graduate school and want to make connections? Reflecting on their goals is the first step to identifying a good program match.

Another important consideration is your student's physical and mental health, especially if they have any preexisting conditions, dietary restrictions, or allergies. If your student is receiving medical or mental health care in the United States, think about how they will continue their care abroad. Many countries have restrictions against certain medications or dosages that are common in the U.S. At this early stage, students should identify a program that limits their exposure to particular health risks, ensures access to local providers who speak English, and allows them to get their essential medications.

Students with disabilities may have unique challenges to study abroad. For example, older infrastructure abroad may mean there are buildings with no elevators. Cobblestone streets could cause issues with mobility. A student with a learning disability who receives more time for tests at their home university may find that accommodation is rare in some countries. Students who rely on access service professionals or service animals will need to thoroughly research their options for traveling with these support providers. Students with disabilities will need to clearly communicate their needs, understand local social perspectives regarding their disability, and ensure appropriate accommodations can be provided before committing to a program.

Students should also consider how elements of their identity could affect their international experience. For example, some countries may not be safe or welcoming for members of the LGBTQ+ community. Heritage seekers—students hoping to use study abroad as a way to explore their family history and culture—expecting to return to the country of their family roots and connect on a deeper level with the local community may feel more out of place than expected.

Another aspect to consider is the overseas learning environment. In the U.S., learning is active; students are encouraged to engage in knowledge creation and participate in class discussions. But in some countries, the professor is the authority with all the knowledge, and students are expected to listen and absorb. In the U.S., final grades are usually made up of several smaller assignments done during the course of the term, but overseas the final grade might be based on one paper or exam. Experiencing a new educational environment is a fascinating way to experience a country's cultural values in action, but your student should be honest about their individual learning style or be ready to adapt.

Prior to choosing a program and location, your student should reflect on their goals and the challenges they may face abroad. Conducting thorough research on their region and program of interest will help ensure your student has appropriate expectations and finds a welcoming community with a balance of challenge and support.

Types of Programs

There are many types of study abroad programs. Short-term programs are typically six weeks or less and often take place in the summer or during spring or winter break. Long-term programs last an academic quarter, semester, or year. Your student's goals will help them determine what level of cultural immersion they prefer. Some programs are more culturally immersive, inviting your student to live like a local, practice the language, take courses with local students, and perhaps board with a host family. Less immersive programs might be shorter in duration, conducted all in English, or involve travel with other Americans. Here are some common program types and their characteristics:

Faculty-Led

Faculty-led means a home university faculty member is teaching a course in the home university curriculum that includes a brief travel experience. They recruit a small group of students from their university to participate. These programs are typically short-term, feature group activities and events, and are less culturally immersive. They are good for students who can't fit a longer experience into their curriculum and who prefer a more scheduled and guided experience.

Exchange

Exchange programs occur when a student's home university partners with an overseas institution. Your student enrolls in the host institution's courses for a semester and often takes courses in the local language with local students, while paying their home university tuition. These programs are especially good for students who have traveled internationally in the past and are looking to develop language skills and be more independent.

Global Campus

Some American universities have a campus abroad. This international satellite location may be exclusive for study abroad students or it may also offer home university degree programs to local students. Traveling to a home school's global campus is a seamless way to study abroad, because courses, faculty, and costs are usually well-integrated with the home program.

Affiliate/Partner

Your student's home university may also partner with affiliates to offer programs. Affiliates are companies, organizations, or other universities that organize study abroad experiences. These partnerships allow universities to offer more flexible locations and course offerings. These programs are accredited, but a student will need to work closely with their academic advisors to make sure the courses taken abroad will count toward their degree program. Affiliates offer other benefits, such as in-country staff support; built-in cultural excursions; scholarships; and more housing options, such as dorms, apartments, or homestays.

Scholarship or Fellowship

Your student should also explore nationally competitive study abroad fellowships. These prestigious programs are often designed and offered by governments or nonprofit organizations and are usually fully funded. Examples include the Fulbright UK Summer Institute, Fulbright Canada Mitacs Globalink, and the DAAD RISE.

Experiential Learning Opportunities

Your student may also participate in international programs that include, or are exclusively designed around, internships, research, or service learning. These can be excellent ways to explore a culture from different viewpoints, gain valuable skills, and contribute to the local community.

When to Go

The earlier your student can have conversations with their faculty, academic advisors, and study abroad office about their interest in studying abroad, the better. Planning a year or more in advance can help a student save more flexible credits (like elective, introductory, or general education credits) for an international experience, which will give them more flexibility and choice in where and when they can go and at what cost. Your student's academic advisor will be most helpful in determining the best time to travel. Study abroad application deadlines are usually three to six months before departure. Scholarship deadlines may be even earlier.

Closing Advice

It may be tempting to let your own fears, concerns, or assumptions overshadow the conversation about study abroad. But you can support your student as they navigate a complicated process and make a financial commitment. Help them reflect on their goals and think about the types of questions they should be asking. Many home universities offer study abroad resources for parents, such as websites, handbooks, or virtual information sessions. Parents are often welcome to join advising or pre-departure meeting, and many global offices are happy to connect you with other parents who've been through this experience. One of the perks might be getting to go abroad yourself and visit your student! You could travel as a family right before or right after your student's program, and there is nothing quite as satisfying as observing their excitement, curiosity, and confidence in their new role as a global citizen.

> ### Conversation Starters
>
> - It sounds like your college has many study abroad options; is this something you would consider?
> - What do you want to get out of a study abroad experience?
> - Have you talked to your academic advisor about the best time to go?
> - Have you thought about how [your allergy, dietary restriction, mobility, etc.] might affect your experience abroad?
> - What are you doing to research your country?
> - How can I support you as you make this decision?

Chapter 6

WHEN SHOULD MY STUDENT START BUILDING THEIR RESUME?

How to prepare for the job search through campus opportunities

Joni O'Hagan
St. John's University

Michelle Kyriakides, Ed.D.
Hofstra University

One of the greatest myths about college to career transitions is that a major defines a student's professional path. Employers often look at skills and abilities as they relate to a position, not the major itself, when determining who to bring in for interviews.

Building a resume is a process that begins from a student's earliest days on campus. Encourage your student to develop the competencies established by the National Association of Colleges and Employers (NACE) as most important based on research with employers. These are:

- Career and self-development
- Communication

- Critical thinking
- Equity and inclusion
- Leadership
- Professionalism
- Teamwork
- Technology

In this chapter, we will explore ideas for how your student can develop confidence with each of the competencies through activities on and off campus.

Career and Self Development

Understanding our interests, skills, and values is essential to identifying the majors, careers, and pathways that will bring us joy, happiness, and, ultimately, success. College offers a much wider array of options than were available in high school. As your student enters their second year of college, they have already taken a few courses through which they have started to identify the subjects that they find more interesting and those in which they struggle.

College is a time to engage in self-discovery. Your student should use the resources available to them to stay on track toward graduation, while also ensuring they pursue a course of study that aligns with their talents. If they are struggling with putting their thoughts about majors and career options into words, their academic and career advisors can help with interest and career assessments and explain the experiential learning opportunities offered at their institution. There are a variety of opportunities for your student to gain experience, build competencies, and develop their resume.

The most common way is through internships. While some internships are not offered until later on in a student's academic program, especially if these are required of the major and result in academic credit, internships that are offered for pay (hourly or a stipend) are not all limited to a student's last year in school. In fact, many employers will advertise early identification programs for first- or second-year students. Your student's career services or academic advisor can help with navigating the options.

Micro, or short-term, internships are paid, project-based opportunities that involve assignments that might be asked of interns or new employees. Micro internships provide a terrific opportunity for students to develop skills and competencies they've identified as an area of growth. And because micro internships typically require a smaller time commitment per week than a traditional internship, students can engage in more opportunities throughout their college experience. Other opportunities your student can explore include job shadowing, case or pitch competitions, hackathons, and leadership days.

A good experience is one that results in a student making a more informed choice. Sometimes that means affirmation that a type of job or perhaps a company is a good fit, and other times it means discovering that the pathway is not one that your student wants to pursue. Either way, the time spent was beneficial.

Communication

Communication has consistently been a skill highlighted in job descriptions and requested by employers who are seeking to hire college graduates. Most often we think about public speaking. However, employers seek a broader scope, including skills in writing, listening, asking questions, and even being aware of yours and others' body language and other nonverbal communication.

If your student is not confident in public speaking, taking a public speaking course is a great way to gain experience, tips, and feedback.

Students should seek out classes that encourage group discussion, so they get used to speaking in group settings as well. They could join a student organization and challenge themselves to speak up in meetings. Do these things sound scary to your student? All the more reason they should take the opportunity in college to become more comfortable.

Developing effective oral communication skills includes developing rapport with individuals. Students can practice this by visiting faculty during their office hours, working on a group project with classmates, or attending networking events. They may even want to get involved in student government and use their voice to advocate for change.

Most colleges have courses that are considered writing-intensive. These courses help to strengthen a student's ability to express themselves succinctly and persuasively—skills that are transferable to many postcollege work environments. Using resources on campus like the writing center will help enhance these skills.

If your student is strong academically, applying for a job in the college's tutoring center is another great way to develop communication skills. Tutors learn how to listen to other students' concerns and then share complex ideas in a simpler format, which is a valuable skill in a variety of career fields.

As students participate in shadowing programs or intern within their field, they also learn how people communicate within their industry. Is it common to use Microsoft Teams, Slack, or email? What's the preferred communication method for various types of messages in the workplace? Asking a mentor for advice can help with these questions.

Critical Thinking

The college experience provides students with many opportunities to build their ability to think critically. For example, while many students believe the career fair is an event for students in their junior or senior year, it might be helpful to your first- or second-year student as they explore career options. Perhaps they identify a company that indicates they are seeking skills your student has not yet honed. Attending the event early provides them time to think about ways to help build those abilities.

Your student might attend the campus activities fair to gather information on clubs and organizations, synthesize those that align with their goals, and consider joining or taking on a leadership role. Or they might pursue and apply for faculty-led research opportunities. Another incredible opportunity in college is the ability to expand one's worldview. While in college, students can take courses that challenge them to think and question, attend political debates or programs that offer new perspectives, take elective courses that develop skills (e.g., technology, public speaking, languages), and engage in conversations that challenge them to see things through a different lens.

Equity and Inclusion

The work world is increasingly diverse, and our students must learn how to communicate with people from different racial and ethnic backgrounds, religions, abilities, cultures, gender identities, sexual orientations, and ages. College campuses are a great place to learn and explore new cultures and meet people who are different from them. Encourage your student to attend events on campus that celebrate diversity and different customs and learn about their history.

As you read about in Chapter 5, study abroad is a terrific way to learn more about a different culture. Living abroad allows students to be immersed in a new culture and challenges them to step outside of their comfort zone. If studying abroad isn't a possibility, then perhaps your student can get involved with helping international students with their adjustment to campus life.

Another great way to learn about diverse viewpoints is to volunteer within the community. Volunteering can take many forms: working with children through literacy initiatives, serving in a soup kitchen, or learning about an issue and advocating for change through political channels. There are offices that provide volunteer experiences on campus and in the community.

Similar to other competencies, we encourage students to explore classes to take for their electives or core requirements that stretch their thinking and force them to explore other viewpoints. Are there opportunities to take classes in LGBTQ+, disability, or gender studies? World religions? Asian studies? Black history? Latin American studies? Encourage your student to talk to their academic advisor about ways to incorporate diversity into their course schedule.

Leadership

Business majors aren't the only ones who need leadership. Leadership is also found in health care, education, sciences, and the creative fields. The ability to influence others, make decisions, solve problems, and communicate with people inside and outside an organization is essential to the world of work.

Encourage your student to seek opportunities to actively learn and practice leadership. They could:

- **Participate in leadership development programs.** Many schools offer programs that lead to certificates. These programs often include workshops and other events that expose students to concepts of leadership and professional facilitators and speakers.

- **Assume leadership roles in campus organizations.** Your student doesn't have to be in a preprofessional organization to develop competencies and connections, though for some majors these preprofessional organizations provide access to alumni, upper-level students, and hands-on experiences like live productions and student-managed investment funds.
- **Seek out mentor opportunities.** Many institutions provide a variety of leadership roles in the form of peer-to-peer mentoring. Some programs are focused on academic success and others on transition to college. Any practice of mentoring helps develop leadership.
- **Take on the role of leader in class assignments and projects.** Leading a team of peers to stay on track and complete a project is not easy, but it will certainly help your student develop leadership skills like time and people management, listening, clear communication, and motivation.

Professionalism

The recent past has seen the traditional work world change significantly. The appropriateness of attire, language and abbreviations, emojis, etc. are constantly in question. Understanding what makes a work environment different from college and demonstrating good work habits are the goals of developing a sense of professionalism.

One of the best ways to become familiar with a professional environment is to work part-time while in school. Encourage your student to assess how a job opportunity aligns with and allows them to build skills toward their career goals. For example, if your student is majoring in hospitality, perhaps a position at a front desk or one that involves customer interaction would be a great fit.

Working on campus is a wonderful opportunity for students. The benefit of on-campus employment is that schedules will be flexible, supervisors are generally understanding of academic and campus commitments, and often students find the department or office in which they work becomes a "home" on campus, with supportive staff and fellow students building a sort of community.

As part of their financial aid package, your student may have received Federal Work-Study, which means that your student is granted an amount of money they can earn by working on campus. Students are paid hourly for work-study positions just like any other student working on campus.

In addition to seeking part-time work, your student, in becoming a professional, should devote time to developing their personal brand and knowledge about their desired industry. Your student might start developing their online presence, selecting a professional profile picture, crafting a LinkedIn headline that stands out, and updating their experience each semester. Online, they should use social media and other news outlets to stay abreast of current events, because it's a good idea to feel comfortable and prepared to discuss news related to their career field. You never know when you might meet your new boss.

A great way to begin building competence within one's industry, and a great resume-builder, is to identify professional associations within the field, join as a student member, and perhaps attend conferences or meetings. Building a network is incredibly important for making connections that may help your student land their first job in their chosen career.

Finally, your student should start preparing their wardrobe for career events and interviews, ensuring they have a few business casual options and some more professional pieces to wear to career fairs, academic events, employer events, and interviews.

Teamwork

Teamwork is an essential part of most businesses and organizations. Students must learn to interact with others from various backgrounds, demonstrate responsibility toward achieving a team goal, meet deadlines, manage conflict effectively through compromise, recognize their own and team members' strengths and weaknesses, and develop strong relationships with peers and supervisors.

Class projects and assignments allow students to practice these skills. Sometimes this is a frustrating experience, because not all students have the same level of commitment to their schoolwork. Learning to navigate these situations, express their concerns, and create a functioning team that turns in the deliverables is part of the learning process.

College students also have the opportunity to develop strong teamwork skills through campus employment opportunities, intramural sports, student organizations, student government, and volunteer work. Each of these opportunities provides students the chance to work with others toward a common goal.

Technology

The one guarantee with technology is that it's constantly changing. Depending on your student's field of study and industry of interest, there are likely software or hardware skills that are required, which can be learned in the classroom or through internships. Adaptability and demonstrating willingness to learn and use new technology is key. Your student will be expected to think about ways that technology can be used to enhance a process or make operations more efficient.

Your student should explore whether their school offers opportunities for certificate programs through coursework or extracurricular offerings. Some schools offer resources that provide students training for free or at a reduced cost. Encourage your student to ask faculty or advisors about what's available.

Your student should also check out job descriptions in their field. What are the key tech skills that are needed? Do they have access to licenses within the school computer labs to practice on their own and develop skills? Employers look at resumes for specific skills, so it's important that students have those key technical skills on their resume.

Campus Career Centers

Your student has gotten involved on campus, volunteered, and taken courses that have helped them develop skills. So now what? Encourage them to visit the campus career center. Advisors can help your student start a resume, draft a cover letter, practice interviewing, and find alumni in their field of interest to help them build their network. Some career centers offer assessments to help students identify areas of interest or take skill inventories, which can help students learn about and articulate their value proposition to employers or set realistic goals for gaining skills. Encourage your student to schedule an appointment or stop by the center to learn more about the resources available.

Closing Advice

It is never too early for your student to think about how college experiences will add to their resume and support their future job search. A campus job is a great place to start, but students should not discount volunteer experiences, organization involvement and leadership positions, and awards/honors received. Your student should take advantage of the opportunities in college to develop the career and life skills that will be needed later.

Conversation Starters

- What resources does the career center on your campus provide?
- Where are alumni from your program working? How do you plan to connect with them?
- What clubs/organizations have you joined on campus?
- What interesting classes have you taken that have exposed you to new ideas or cultures?
- What events on campus have you attended? Did you learn anything?
- What's been the greatest challenge working on group projects?

Chapter 7

HOW MIGHT MY STUDENT CHANGE DURING COLLEGE?

How to prepare for your student's identity exploration

Maureen Hurley
Emerson College

Students change and develop at a remarkable rate during the roughly four years of college, similar to the first four years of life. As a toddler, your child tried on identities within the family. As a sophomore in college, your student may try on identities to see what works in terms of being an individual in society and the world. Often, students will experiment with appearance—an edgy haircut or piercings, for example. Other students may be exploring their religious beliefs, sexuality, or their vision of themselves in the future.

Supporting your sophomore through these explorations might be challenging for you and your family. For some families, the identity shift will not come as a surprise; for others, it might be brand-new territory. This chapter will help you to prepare for these challenges and provide questions and strategies to help begin discussions.

Appearance

Appearance is a well-documented area of experimentation for students. Tattoo parlors are common near college campuses for a reason—students are eager to get inked. It's worthwhile to discuss in advance how you feel about permanent tattoos. Of course, it is the student's choice whether or not to use their body as a canvas, but some families might prefer to be a part of the process rather than be surprised. It is even fairly common for parents to accompany their student to the studio. They sometimes even pay for the tattoo! Are you fine with a tattoo as long as it is a good-quality one or if it cannot be easily seen? Talk in advance about your comfort level and find out how it aligns with your student's ideas. It might be appropriate to talk about how a choice made today may not be desirable in the future. Your student might want to declare love for a partner in a tattoo, assuming the relationship will last longer than the college years. These choices sometimes result in expensive and painful removal procedures if the relationship dissolves. Scrupulous tattoo artists will counsel students away from these choices, but conversations with parents can also help students make a decision they won't later regret.

Is it important to you that your student is not picking the bargain tattoo parlor? That they've done research and are not getting tattooed as a dare or on a whim? There are a wide variety of options in choosing a tattoo parlor. Some use the most sophisticated cleaning and sterilization techniques imaginable, and others are more lax. A tattoo should be met with as much consideration as a medical procedure. As there is a fair risk of infection, you'll want to ask your student if they know the hygienic way to care for the tattoo. There are some medical considerations, too. For example, if your student has an illness or condition that requires frequent MRI imaging, a medical doctor might want to weigh in on the choice of a tattoo. Because the ink contains metal, it may cause complications with MRIs. Tattoo parlors are not regulated federally, but all states require a student to be 18 prior to getting inked.

Piercings are another body decoration that many college-age students choose. These have many of the same safety concerns as tattooing and, although they are not always as difficult to reverse as tattoos, they should be considered permanent. The piercings and tattoos referred to in this chapter fall under the umbrella of adornment and not of the more extreme expression known as body modification.

Unlike tattoos, haircuts and hair dyes are not permanent, and they may not spark intense feelings for the family. It is common to see hair colors that don't exist in nature on a college campus. Gender-neutral haircuts, such as shaved heads and man buns, are sometimes meant to have shock value, and other times they signal that the student is trying on a new identity, as you might try on a new coat. A casual approach to an appearance change will help to let your student know that you see the person below the mohawk as the same person they were before.

The same philosophy applies to wardrobe and style choices. As long as the student knows that sweatpants and a pink mohawk won't be the best choice for most (but not all) job interviews, you will likely be reassured. Talk through these choices in a nonjudgmental manner so you can understand what your student is thinking with their decisions. Asking them if they plan on growing out their natural hair color in the future is likely to be more productive than a heated conversation about whether or not the purple and green hair will cause a heart attack in a loved one. Nonpermanent explorations of hair, makeup, and clothing probably won't rise to the level of causing conflict, but if they do, again, a conversation about why the student is choosing the style can spark a conversation about your child's creative identity.

Religious Expression

Choices that students make, such as how to express their religious beliefs, may weigh heavily on parents who perhaps hold a different value. It is not uncommon for students to explore other religions, different expressions of spirituality, and even to completely abandon a religious practice that parents considered an integral part of family life. As difficult as it may be, have a discussion with your student about why they have made this choice. Listen to your student; if your student feels listened to and understood, they may be more likely to listen to your point of view.

Remember that a significant element of education is to learn to question everything. Interacting with people from diverse backgrounds and differing ideas helps the student find the direction they want to grow. Religious exploration can eventually lead to a deeper understanding of one's own upbringing and faith. Framing this type of choice as a developmentally appropriate exploration rather than early-adult rebellion makes going through it much easier. If your student is joining a different religion than the family, ask about it. Why is your student drawn to this practice? What can they tell you about it? If they no longer wish to be part of a religious practice at home, such as going to church, ask questions about why, and try to listen to the answers. If churchgoing is a family practice, ask that your student accompany you when they are home out of respect for you. If they cannot agree, let them know that you will ask each time they are home because it is important to you.

If you feel that there is an element of the new religion that strikes you as being cultlike, it is appropriate to learn more. Cults do not let people choose to leave the group. They typically require more and more time from participants and often require larger and larger financial contributions. Cults often prey on students who have not created close relationships in college, on international students, and on those with depression or other mental health concerns. If you feel that your student has become involved in a religious group that may be harmful, it may be appropriate to contact a campus chaplain or office for spiritual life to let them know about the situation and ask for advice on how to support your student.

Sexual Orientation and Gender Identity

Some explorations are not choices, but rather expressions of identity that students discover. These identities typically have to do with emerging sexuality. For example, many students come out as lesbian, gay, bisexual, transgender, or queer (LGBTQ+) during the college years. For many LGBTQ+ students, coming out is an acknowledgement of what they have felt on the inside for some time, and college may be when they have the first opportunity to express this aspect of their identity. For parents, this identity may not be a surprise at all, or it could be a shock to the entire family.

If this news is distressing, you will likely need to have some time to process the information. Either way, your student will need to know that your love is a constant. Sharing this identity with you is an act of supreme trust on the part of your student, and letting them know that you always love them is so important.

Coming out as transgender, in particular, is brave and very difficult for the entire family. It is a rewiring of the vision held—by student and parents—of what the future would look like. Acceptance does not mean perfectly using the preferred pronoun every time, but trying to. It does not mean destroying every photo and artifact of the student's previous identity, but it might mean packing them away for a while.

We know that LGBTQ+ students are up to four times more likely to attempt suicide than cisgender, heterosexual students. The self-harm is not due to having an LGBTQ+ identity, but rather the fear of not being accepted in their family, college community, and society at large. Keeping your LGBTQ+ student safe begins with admissions of love. Most campuses have LGBTQ+ offices, student organizations, and counseling groups. Help your student locate them. Avoid organizations that claim to convert LGBTQ+ people. Lastly, let your student tell you their truth at their own pace. A student might dip a toe into the water with a disclosure to gauge your reaction, but then not want to go into a deeper conversation. That is okay. They are looking to see how you will react to the news. Let them tell you more when they are ready.

Family Support

All explorations being made by your student may come with a feeling of loss for you. This can be as simple as your former carnivore now eschewing family barbecue time, or as life-altering as your child coming out as transgendered. You can grieve the loss of the future you envisioned, but taking an interest in the exploration—whether it be making a recipe with your newly minted vegan, going to a service at a new church, or attending a gay pride parade with your student—is a supportive and lovely way to connect.

There are many resources for families with LGBTQ+ students specifically. Two nationwide organizations are PFLAG (originally Parents and Friends of Lesbians and Gays, but now encompasses anyone in the "queer" spectrum) and Family Equality. These organizations help families to adjust to the identities that their students have shared with them. They offer fellowship and friendship for parents and family members who may be feeling isolated, afraid, and helpless.

Acknowledging your own feelings about your student's expression of identity is important for you to share with another parent, friend, or counselor, but these are not typically helpful to share with your student. Students coming out often have their own trials with acceptance, and hearing about your struggle may not have the impact you intend. Instead, ask questions about how your student feels about their identity, the challenges and celebrations they have experienced, and whether they want to talk about a romantic relationship. You might also ask if they have explored the resources on campus that might support them.

Closing Advice

Parents know that students are going to change and grow during college. Parents want this, crave this, and sometimes fear this. Keeping open lines of communication, asking questions, being willing to try something new, and always starting from a place of unconditional love will go a long way in carrying you and your student through changes in the sophomore year and beyond.

> ### Conversation Starters
>
> - Are you planning on getting haircuts at school or when you are home?
> - Do many students get tattoos or piercings? What are your thoughts about permanent appearance changes? Will you let me know what you decide to do?
> - What does your faith practice look like when you're at school? Are you okay with still coming to services with us when you are home?
> - Can you tell me what the climate on campus is like for LGBTQ+ students?

Chapter 8
SHOULD I WORRY ABOUT MY STUDENT'S WELL-BEING?

How to encourage self-care and wellness

Carrie Glatting
RMHCI, Orlando

Samantha Jeffries, LMFT
Rochester Institute of Technology

At this point in your student's academic journey, you are likely no stranger to the fact that college is a stressful time for students and parents. While your student deals with the ups and downs of college life, you are left watching, often from afar, as your student works to manage everything. As you may have experienced during your student's first year, it can be difficult to balance your desire to provide space for them to grow with that nagging feeling in the back of your mind saying that something just isn't right. So, when do you need to worry about your student's well-being? How do you assess your student's level of functioning when they aren't in front of you?

Even though you would like certainty, things aren't always cut-and-dried when it comes to mental health and well-being. There are going to be moments (probably many!) when you worry about your student, only to find out that everything is completely fine. Alternatively, there will be moments when your worries and concerns are spot-on. Know that it is completely normal to worry about your student.

This chapter will explore some of the indicators that might signal that your student is struggling. Keep in mind that these indicators are meant to be broad and general and may not indicate a problem for every student. You know your student best and should always trust your gut, regardless of what others may or may not view as signs of struggle.

Common Mental Health Concerns

It's not only normal but expected that students will experience some mental health struggles during college; these are challenging years. One of the primary things to look for is a persistent change in your student's patterns or baseline level of functioning. Your student may have always experienced social anxiety, and college life could exacerbate it a bit, but if their behavioral pattern hasn't changed, then the symptoms you see may be less concerning. Noticing a lack of engagement and more negative thinking for a student who has always been a highly motivated and positive person is something to pay closer attention to.

Here are some of the common mental health concerns commonly seen at college:

Preexisting Concerns

Preexisting concerns are diagnoses that you and your student are aware of prior to the start of their sophomore year. Common examples include eating disorders, ADHD, autism spectrum disorder, depression, and anxiety, as well as many medical diagnoses. Work with your student in advance to ensure that they have an appropriate treatment plan in place while they are away. Who is providing them treatment while they are at school? Are you noticing any signs that your student's preexisting concern may be worsening? Did they struggle with any mental health concerns that went untreated in their first year?

Generalized Anxiety Disorder (GAD)

GAD is one of the most common mental health diagnoses. Its hallmark is persistent and uncontrollable worry about a number of different things, so the worries and anxiety are not always focused on the same thing all the time. Someone struggling with GAD may appear to bounce from worry to worry and have a difficult time letting go of their anxieties. Additional symptoms indicative of GAD can include:

- Irritability
- Difficulty sleeping and increased fatigue
- Inability to focus
- Lack of communication or an inability to bring oneself to respond to communications
- Physical symptoms such as nausea, sweating, or change in appetite

Social Anxiety

All the unknowns and unfamiliar situations associated with college create the perfect storm for students to develop social anxiety. While you might expect this to develop more during your student's first year of college, a lot of students return to campus for their sophomore year and begin to develop social anxiety or deal with social anxiety from the previous year. Even if your student appears to feel more settled heading into their sophomore year, keep in mind that college is a constantly changing environment. Students are faced with new floormates, new classmates, new teammates. Signs that your student may be struggling with social anxiety include:

- Crippling fear of social interactions and situations in which one might feel judged
- Avoidance of social situations due to fear of anticipated judgment or embarrassment

Depression

Depression is another incredibly common mental health diagnosis, and it presents itself in a multitude of ways. You may have seen some symptoms of depression in your student last year, or you might just be noticing that something feels a little off this year. Depression can appear to be cyclical for some students, arising at more difficult points in the semester such as midterms/finals or returning from break and decreasing at more positive points. Other students may appear to struggle with symptoms of depression throughout the semester or year. Some signs that your student may be struggling with depression include:

- Feeling down or "blue"
- Feeling hopeless or helpless
- Lacking interest or desire to engage in activities that they once enjoyed
- Sleeping too much and not being able to get out of bed
- Isolating themselves; not communicating with others
- Self-harming behaviors or expressing suicidal thoughts
- Engaging in substance abuse
- Lacking direction, time management skills, and motivation

Holistic Health

We often think of holistic wellness as nutrition, exercise, and sleep, but there are additional activities that help develop healthy life skills. Many colleges and universities have adopted nine dimensions of wellness as a guide to support students. These dimensions—physical, emotional, creative, environmental, financial, occupational, intellectual, social, and spiritual—are ideals, not standards or fixed goals, and illustrate what wellness looks like for everyday college life. For example, when we seek out musical activities and cultural experiences, we're enhancing our creative wellness. When we take a budgeting course or attend a FAFSA workshop, we are increasing our sense of financial wellness. Below are a couple of examples of how supporting students using these nine dimensions fosters their holistic success. You can read more about these dimensions in the next chapter (see page 78).

Financial Wellness

Students who experience stress over finances in college find it difficult to attend social events that cost money or lose sleep over worry about how they will pay for books, and that stress can often impact their class participation and grades. If you know your student is struggling with financial wellness, encourage them to meet with a financial aid representative. There may be additional grants, scholarships, and work-study opportunities available to close the financial need gap. Academic departments often offer scholarships within a major, so encourage your student to talk with their advisor. You can also help them establish a college budget to manage their money and help them explore campus employment opportunities. Additionally, college campuses have many free events for students, providing social opportunities at no cost.

Social Wellness

Social connections, both positive and negative, can have a direct impact on physical health, emotional well-being, and academics. Students who struggle to connect with their peers may find that they begin to feel isolated, are not engaging in self-care, and feel less engaged with their academics. Social wellness can often improve after the first year, but it doesn't always. Your student might say things like:

- "I'm not connecting with my roommate this year."
- "There aren't any events on campus that I'm interested in."
- "Everyone is already in a clique."
- "I just don't fit in here."

For some parents, the immediate reaction to hearing thoughts like these is to call the student affairs office on campus and inquire how to improve this situation. While reaching out to your student's college with a concern can be helpful, we want to encourage you first to pause, let your student know you are glad they came to you with this problem, and then ask how they would like to proceed or solve the problem. You can ask more leading questions, such as, "What are other ways you might find friends with similar interests as you?" Give them time to come up with a response without making your own suggestions and trying to solve the problem.

Prioritizing Self-Care and Advocacy

Your student is in their second year of college now; surely, after a year of independence, they have figured out how to care for themselves and advocate for their own needs, right? Not always! While these skills may come naturally to some students, others struggle with recognizing their needs, addressing them, and then advocating for themselves with professors, providers, and campus staff.

Sometimes this lack of self-care will be visible to you, like if you're video chatting with your student and notice that they don't appear to be brushing their hair, changing their clothes, or getting enough rest. It's pretty obvious in that moment that self-care has taken a bit of a back seat, and you will want to check in with them about how they are doing. In less obvious moments, your student will have to tell you if they are struggling and having a difficult time reaching out to available support services. You may notice that your student doesn't seem as motivated as they usually are, they aren't reaching out to you as often as they usually do, or they might hint that they aren't going to class and completing assignments. It can be frustrating to know that your student is having a difficult time and either can't, or won't, reach out to the resources available to them that could help.

At times, that old instinct from your student's younger years may kick in and you'll want to call the college, their counselor, or their advisor and start advocating for them. It's important to remember, however, that part of the college experience is learning how to not only care for yourself, but also to advocate for what you need, learning also how to accept disappointment in moments when those wants or needs cannot be met. As you and your student prepare for their sophomore year, it can be helpful to spend time reflecting on their first year by asking questions such as:

- What behavior patterns could be improved upon this year?
- What are some ways in which you struggled to care for yourself or speak up when you needed support?
- Are there resources or support services that you can connect to earlier in the semester to avoid some of the pitfalls of last year?

Resilience

Remember when your student was younger and missed the final shot that cost the team the playoff? Or when your student worked for months on an art project and wasn't selected for the gallery show? What about their first breakup? Do you recall how your student coped during those experiences? Did they pout around the house for several days or weeks? Did they get right back out to the court and practice? Those experiences were building their resiliency and preparing them for college life. Resiliency is the capacity to withstand or to recover from difficulties. Parents often want to remove pain and disappointment from their children's lives because they don't like to see them hurting. However, hurt is an opportunity for growth and the development of resiliency skills.

Higher education professionals are seeing an increase in the number of students coming to college lacking resilience and problem-solving skills. Some students earn a poor grade on a test and decide that, because they're going to fail the class, they might as well stop attending. This action makes it more difficult to recover. Students with strong problem-solving skills will take steps to improve their grade by talking to the professor, going to the tutoring center, or using a study buddy in the class. Another example is with illness. When students don't notify their professors about missing class, they miss assignments or attendance points. They also may not take care of themselves and end up with a longer recovery period because they didn't go to the health center, find a way to get food, or get needed prescriptions. Emailing a professor or picking up medications may sound like simple tasks (after all, you likely email your boss and make a pharmacy run when you are sick), but these are life skills that students likely didn't have to learn before being on their own in college. It is not appropriate for you to contact your student's professor to ask for assignment extensions if they are sick, but you should help your student understand the importance of doing so.

Share Your Stories

Sharing your own difficult experiences normalizes the reality that struggle, challenge, and even failure, are a natural part of life. Talk about how you got fired from a job and what steps you took to get another one. Let your student know if you had to take chemistry three times before you finally passed, and what steps you took to improve your grades each time. Tell your student about the strained relationship with your coach that led to your college transfer after your first year. Did you struggle with weight or anxiety in your 20s? These are important conversations that can develop deeper connections with your student and more awareness around family medical history. In the age of social media and reality shows, we don't always get to see what real struggle, challenge, and failure look like. We realize that many students come to college having lived through plenty of difficult experiences. Some students understand resilience more than we would like them to. All parents want their students to be able to talk about difficult experiences and know that they are not alone.

Closing Advice

Although your sophomore has a year of college under their belt, they will still encounter new challenges and will look to you for reminders and support. Your student is going to call you. They are going to lean on you. They are going to look to you for guidance. Be prepared to listen, to pause, to refrain from solving problems for them, and, most importantly, to share your own stories with them.

Conversation Starters

- What's your plan for treatment of your preexisting concern?

- What are some changes you'd like to make your second year in school better?

- Are you experiencing any depression or anxiety? What can I do to help?

- What are some ways you can cope with challenges? What has worked for you in the past?

- Have you thought about any challenges that might come up for you this second year?

Chapter 9

HOW WILL I KNOW IF SOMETHING IS WRONG?

How to recognize signs of struggle

Trish Moser and Penelope Strater
Rollins College

As parents and family supporters of sophomores, it is not uncommon to receive stressful calls or texts from your student expressing feelings of frustration, sadness, anxiety, or being overwhelmed, especially during the fall semester of the second year. Sophomores can continue to struggle with finding their fit socially and academically on campus. They may not be enjoying required courses, friends they met during their first year may not have developed a lasting bond, high school relationships may have changed, or their campus may not be as diverse as expected. This chapter will help you see signs of the sophomore slump.

Recognizing Signs of Struggle

The sophomore slump does not just affect students who have previously struggled; it can affect students who did well their first year, as things become more difficult and routines start to shift. Stress for sophomore students can manifest as anxiety, depression, and other worrying behaviors. Students can feel a sense of pressure to do better academically than their first year, or pressure to choose a major when they have yet to decide upon their academic or career goals. Your student may not feel as much support on their campus, because they are no longer part of a first-year program that provided a network of peer leaders, a cohort-based experience, or a first-year advisor. Higher education institutions typically have strong first-year programs, but not as many campuses offer structured programs for sophomore students. This means that sophomores can sometimes feel lost or unmotivated after the first-year support has disappeared.

During their sophomore year, students also experience growing internal questions about life purpose and college persistence. For example, your student (or family) may have had long-held dreams about a particular major and career path, and this dream may be changing as new passions are discovered. As they reconsider major or career choices, it is not uncommon for sophomore students to start thinking they should transfer to another institution or even withdraw altogether, rather than consider the options available to them. Similar to the potential identity shifts you read about in Chapter 7, students identify strongly with their major and career goals, and changing their plans can cause stress and confusion.

If you receive stressful calls or frantic texts from your student, understand that you are most likely on the receiving end of an emotional release from your student. As a family member receiving this type of call or text, your first step should be to be a good listener. Remind your student that what they are feeling is a part of the regular ups and downs of college life, and they are not alone in feeling this way. This is a very important point and worth repeating whenever your student faces a new challenge.

Specific behaviors to listen for when communicating with your student include:

- Failing to attend regular classes
- Turning in assignments late
- Lacking motivation
- Ignoring deadlines
- Showing general unhappiness about social connections and academic life

These are signs that your student may need some additional support from you and campus resources.

Engaging with and Supporting Your Student

Parents are often the first call a student makes when they encounter a problem or concern. The first thing you should consider when this happens is whether your student is able to solve this problem on their own. Remember that emotions will be high and you do not need to immediately react. They may just need a listening ear or your support in finding resources and a solution. Allowing your student to lead this conversation and work through the issue gives them the opportunity to practice problem-solving, decision-making, self-advocacy, and relationship-building. These skills help students deal constructively with life challenges and develop a sense of independence that will set them up for success in adulthood.

Here are some specific steps to take when supporting your student through a challenging situation:

Take a Breath

Before responding, take a breath and listen to your student. The urge may be to immediately try to fix things for your sophomore, but acknowledge their struggle first. Be sure to:

- Validate: "I'm sorry to hear that you are struggling."
- Appreciate: "I'm glad you told me about this so I can help support you."
- Refer: "What have you tried so far? Let's look up some resources together."

Find Resources

Encourage your student to check their college or university website for resources and help them find campus support as needed. There are countless offices and teams designed to offer guidance and assistance to students in a variety of areas (see page 78 for examples). Campus counseling centers and wellness areas are particularly important for students who continue to struggle after trying other strategies. These offices are designed to address common student issues. They are able to help students find on- and off-campus support as needed.

Embrace Change

Understand that your student will change throughout the college years. Don't stress if they no longer want to be a doctor or want to try out interests they've never expressed before. Your student may hesitate telling you about such changes out of fear of disappointing you, but letting them know you are there for them will open up lines of communication. Give your student and yourself time and space to acknowledge and accept changes.

Expect and Support Changing Relationships

As your student continues making new friends in college, relationships will start to change. They will likely start to talk less frequently to friends from home and focus on these new friendships. On the other hand, your student may not have found their people yet. It can take time to find a friend group, and this is very apparent at the start of sophomore year. Getting involved in campus groups (e.g., academic, athletic, service, social) can help them find friends with similar interests and outlooks. Prepare yourself for any ups and downs in this area of their life, and remind them that shifting relationships is completely normal.

Share Problem-Solving Strategies

Developmentally, it is time for your student to solve their own problems and learn to advocate for themselves if they have not already. Problem-solving skills are an essential part of adulthood, and college provides a safe environment to develop this ability and enable their independence. Use this opportunity to pass the baton of adulthood and support your student as they think through options, identify resources, and initiate actions to resolve their dilemmas.

Identifying Resources

As you read in Chapter 8, there are nine commonly held dimensions of wellness: physical, emotional, creative, environmental, financial, occupational, intellectual, social, and spiritual (some literature also incorporates digital wellness as a tenth dimension). Your student may be struggling in one or more of these dimensions and may not even be aware of gaps that are contributing to their struggle. As students learn to advocate for themselves, they must also learn self-awareness in order to understand where these gaps are.

The following chart will help your student find appropriate resources and tools to fulfill those dimensions that are lacking and improve their well-being. Including questions about the different dimensions of wellness in conversations with your student will help them think about their well-being holistically. Once you help your student identify areas that could use support, help them locate campus resources and tools available to meet their needs. Remind your student that they are not alone, and these campus resources exist specifically to meet their wellness needs and support their overall academic success. Most colleges and universities have departments, resources, and tools to meet all dimensions of student wellness. Here are examples for each dimension:

Dimension	Resources
Physical Wellness Ensuring self-care through nutrition, exercise, sleep, safe sex, healthy relationships, and medical care	• Student health center • Gym and recreation center • Club sports and intramurals • Wellness programming
Emotional Wellness Coping with stress and expressing emotions effectively	• Counseling center • Case management • Wellness programming
Creative Wellness Expressing self and identity through multiple perspectives	• Clubs and organizations • Dance, theater, and music programming

(continued)

Dimension	Resources
Environmental Wellness Feeling safe and supported in one's surroundings	• Residence life and housing • Public safety • Multicultural center • First-generation office • Off-campus or commuter student center
Financial Wellness Supporting life goals in college and in the future	• Financial aid and scholarships • Student financial services • Student employment • Career services
Occupational Wellness Finding a meaningful career path	• Career services • Student employment • Community engagement • Leadership programming
Intellectual Wellness Achieving academic success and demonstrating learning	• Academic advisors • Tutoring centers • Writing centers • Academic success programming • Libraries

(continued)

Dimension	Resources
Social Wellness Sustaining relationships and successful interaction with others	• Student life • Clubs and organizations • Club sports and intramurals • Multicultural center • First-generation office • Veteran services
Spiritual Wellness Clarifying personal beliefs and life purpose	• Religious and spiritual life centers • Cultural centers • Community engagement • Volunteering opportunities
Digital Wellness Setting healthy boundaries with screen time and technology	• Academic success programming • Community engagement • Clubs and organizations • Club sports and intramurals

Closing Advice

You will most likely receive calls and texts from your student, either in distress or in celebration of a recent accomplishment. The ups and downs of sophomore year are a valuable part of the college experience, as well as your student's transition to adulthood. Successful adults are problem-solvers and have the ability to advocate for themselves. Help your student develop self-awareness, encourage self-advocacy and problem-solving skills, and know that college and university resources are readily available.

Conversation Starters

- In what areas have you been struggling this year?
- How can I support your holistic wellness?
- What have you been doing to stay healthy?
- Which high school friends are you still in contact with?
- How have you engaged in the campus community?

Chapter 10
WHAT DOES IT MEAN TO BE A CAMPUS LEADER?

How to encourage continued engagement

Bridget Guernsey Riordan
Emory University

As students enter college, the question they get most frequently is, "What is your major?" Knowing what they want to study is likely the most significant factor when students choose their college. However, along with academic development, social and personal development are also important. When students take on leadership roles, they help develop strong social and organizational skills. Your support and encouragement of this extracurricular development will go far in your student's holistic development.

By the second year in college, students have learned the landscape of their campus and have a general understanding of cocurricular offerings. They may have joined a few clubs and organizations or participated in service or community activities. Now is a good time to reflect on what they have observed and determine where they want to focus their time and energy. This may mean deciding what groups fuel their passions and which groups do not provide meaningful engagement. Asking your student these questions may help them with values clarification and future direction.

Leadership has many facets and is not about the position a person holds. It is about developing skills, influencing others, and making an impact. Although it may look great to note the role of president on a resume, more important will be to translate what was learned through leadership roles and how that can apply to life after college.

Developing Skills

Through academic study, students become proficient in math, writing, and scientific research, among other skills. With extracurricular experiences, students are exposed to a number of developmental skills that will serve them for a lifetime. These include:

- Written communication
- Oral presentations
- Organizational skills
- Responsibility
- Accountability
- Planning skills
- Leadership within small and large groups
- Meeting management
- Financial management
- Guidance
- Decision-making
- Problem-solving
- Interdependence
- Critical thinking

- Conflict resolution
- Adaptability
- Flexibility
- Empathy

You can help your student by discussing these skills and helping them consider where they have places for improvement and development. From there, they can determine how to shape their college involvement.

It is important for you and your student to remember that college is a learning environment, where students are able to make mistakes, learn from those mistakes, and do better the next time. The stakes may not be as large as they will be when they are in professional positions or graduate school, however, they can learn from trial and error and gain experience from failures as well as successes. Most college organizations have a staff or faculty advisor to help guide students in their decision-making processes. They provide a historical perspective and a moral compass to help make ethical decisions. In addition, older student leaders can offer advice and serve as role models for strong student leadership. Encourage your student to cultivate relationships with mentors and seek out role models. These individuals can provide valuable guidance to emerging leaders.

Not Everyone Can Be President

Not everyone will get elected president, and being president may not offer the best hands-on experiences. Many other opportunities for leadership growth and development exist within organizations and extracurricular experiences. Some of the positions may need a specific level of expertise or interest, like the positions of financial manager, communicator/social media specialist, or fundraising chair. Other positions will offer general learning opportunities, such as alumni relations chair, altruism chair, and social event planner. Students should determine what interests them and where their skills can be of value. They may not need to know every aspect of the role before taking it on, but they should have an idea about how they will learn it and what success will look like.

Opportunities to Acquire Leadership Skills

Service, sports, and social groups offer multiple avenues for students to gain leadership experience. Students can be involved in more than one type of organization and vary their level of involvement based on their interests. They may choose to be an officer in one club, for example, and an active participant in another. In order to balance their curricular and cocurricular commitments, it is wise to limit involvement to organizations where a student can be fully engaged. Talk with your student about not getting overextended and about how to balance involvement so that it is enjoyable, as well as an avenue to gain valuable skills.

Service

One way all students can understand group dynamics, explore their community, and develop leadership skills is through service. Many colleges and universities have designated offices for community service and often sponsor service trips, service days, fall or spring break trips, and opportunities for students to serve on a limited basis. Students can search through service opportunities and determine where they can participate meaningfully. Examples of service include:

- Connecting with seniors or veterans
- Fighting homelessness or hunger
- Tutoring
- Working on environmental sustainability

- Looking out for animal welfare
- Working on social justice issues

Service may be campus-based or located in the neighboring community. Service activities might expose students to national organizations such as Make-a-Wish Foundation or the American Cancer Society and its Relay for Life.

Through serving the community, students continue to learn how their actions can make a difference in improving the world. They also can discover an area to explore that can continue into adulthood. Often, service complements academic work. For example, students in health-related majors may choose to become peer counselors, hospital volunteers, or emergency medical technicians. Prelaw students may volunteer to register voters or serve on a political campaign.

Participating in service allows students to demonstrate that they understand the world beyond themselves and have the maturity and appreciation to volunteer their time and energy. Often, service involves organizing groups, managing projects, and planning events and activities. All of these skills are valued in the workplace. Reinforce this with your student by supporting them in their service efforts and discussing what they have learned and gained from these experiences.

Student Organizations

Joining a student organization can open up multiple possibilities. Student organizations typically have established bylaws, rules, and traditions and complement the mission of the college. First-year students often sign up for multiple organizations and are encouraged to explore every opportunity open to them. Initially, students may join groups out of curiosity or to explore a new interest. After exploring, students can decide what involvement is most meaningful and how they want to focus their energy.

Political Groups

Colleges are known as places for open expression and political discourse. As they approach the legal voting age and take political science classes, students can explore ideology and government through politically based student organizations. Students can canvas the community to encourage voter registration, engage in ideological debates, learn from political experts, or explore international humanitarian efforts. Skills that can be developed include empathy, understanding other cultures, communication, and collaboration. If your student starts to develop political views that are different from yours, you will have lively family discussion. Ask your student why they believe what they do. You may be surprised at what you learn.

Religious Groups

College students may continue following the religious beliefs they were brought up with or begin exploring different faiths and beliefs. This can be difficult for families, so it will take understanding and patience. Religious student organizations usually support the corresponding on-campus or community religious services, provide support for students, and function as a place for discussing and understanding world religions. Students involved with religious organizations can develop skills such as understanding other cultures and practicing empathy, critical thinking, and problem resolution.

Greek Letter Organizations

Greek letter organizations—fraternities and sororities—often focus on service, social interactions, and shared values. Many fraternities and sororities are nationally affiliated, with long histories at their host institutions. Students usually join in their first or second year and continue active membership during their college years and into adulthood, because fraternal and sororal organizations have a network of alumni throughout the country and encourage lifelong involvement.

These organizations offer opportunities to explore many aspects of student life, including service, social activities, event planning, and personal development. They often have a large slate of officers and provide many chances for holding a leadership position. The groups promote alumni networking and community connections. Because they may involve a large financial commitment, you will want to discuss potential membership with your student before they consider joining a group.

Identity and Special Interest Groups

Exploring identity development and special interests is a great opportunity for students to consider who they are and what fuels their passions. Identities may include racial, ethnic, and sexual orientation, and special interests can vary from investing to journalism. With identity development, students learn to understand differences and how identity impacts individuals. Empathy, compassion, interdependence, and conflict resolution can all be gained from exploring issues of identity. Special interest groups help students develop a passion for something that has meaning to them. That may be dance or vocal groups, animal rescue, or sustainability. These groups often lead to strong friendships and relationships, as students gain insights into others and learn interdependence. Encourage your student to explore what excites them and brings them joy. These experiences will offer stress relief and the chance to gain self-confidence and satisfaction.

Sports

Opportunities for student involvement in sports-based or recreational organizations include club sports, intramural sports, and outdoor-interest clubs. Club sports are not part of the National Collegiate Athletic Association (NCAA) but are hosted by the institution and provide a way for students to compete with other students at area colleges and universities. If a student enjoyed playing lacrosse in high school or wants to learn rugby, they can continue that activity or develop it in college. Intramural sports are within the college and often involve competition between residence halls and/or fraternities and sororities. Outdoor-interest clubs can range from mountain climbing to backpacking to ice skating and allow students to explore new activities or continue earlier passions.

All of these sports allow students to practice teamwork, cooperate for a common goal, and enjoy competition and camaraderie—all skills valuable in the workplace. As your student considers stretching themselves physically, discuss safety and precautions with participation, potential transportation issues, and out-of-pocket expenses.

Closing Advice

Leadership development is one of the most important aspects of the collegiate experience. This is a time for students to experiment, branch out, and test themselves. Developing leadership skills can happen in multiple ways in a variety of student organizations and experiences. Families can support their students by encouraging them to get out of their comfort zones, explore varied opportunities, and stretch themselves to take on challenges and learning experiences. The academic side of college is critical, but developing strong leadership skills will be vital in developing a well-rounded student.

Conversation Starters

- What are you really passionate about?
- What new or different cocurricular experiences would you like to explore?
- What leadership skills do you want to develop?
- How can you add value to an organization?
- How much time do you want to devote to cocurricular activities?

Chapter 11

HOW IMPORTANT IS MY STUDENT'S SOCIAL CIRCLE?

How to support an ever-changing social life

Whitney White
University of Cincinnati

Sophomore students typically return to campus with a higher level of comfort and a lower learning curve than their first-year peers. During their second year of college, students continue to solidify their sense of self and belonging, from their involvement on campus to their friendships and romantic relationships. Establishing healthy relationships and finding a community where we feel connected and valued is an essential part of our experience as humans. College gives students many opportunities to develop social skills and learn how to be productive and compassionate members of society. The social circle is an essential part of your student's support system on campus, because their sense of belonging can impact everything from their wellness to their academic success.

Friendships

College student friend groups evolve a lot during the first year as students explore their interests, identity, and involvement opportunities across campus. During the second year, your student may let go of or lessen their investment in some relationships, while choosing to nourish others. These relationship changes come naturally with the experiences that sophomore year brings. Your student will be solidifying who they are and what they want, increasing their depth of involvement in preferred campus activities, and possibly moving off campus.

If your student isn't living in campus residence halls during their second year, building and maintaining relationships can take a little extra work. They may enjoy their newfound privacy but miss the hustle and bustle of the residence halls. They might not have multiple people living right outside their door or university-run social activities happening down the hall. Off-campus residents often go to campus for class and then return to their apartments. Encourage your student to stick around a little longer, by studying in the library, attending an event on campus, or grabbing a bite on campus with a friend. Encourage them to check out the events calendars from their college's student activities offices, multicultural and identity centers, and student unions for upcoming activities and ways to connect with campus and meet new friends.

Building Healthy Friendships

Encourage your student to surround themselves with others who accept, value, and share in their success. We all deserve supportive friends and relationships built on trust, honesty, and respect. And it is equally important to have your student reflect on how they can be a good friend to others. What steps can they take to show care and concern for their friends? How would they step in to provide support if a friend was in trouble? How might they manage conflict with a friend?

Talk to your student about your own relationships. To whom are you closest? What about those relationships makes them so valuable to you? You might want to share how you nourish your own relationships, such as prioritizing spending time together, actively listening to the other person's needs, or apologizing when you are wrong.

High School Friends

Other friendships that may change this year are your student's relationships with their high school friends. Your student likely maintained many of these relationships during the first year and may have reconnected with them at home during the summer. As time goes on, these relationships are often replaced by deepening college friendships. Your student's college friends are there every day, connecting with them around their current interests and sharing in the journey to adulthood. If your student is concerned about evolving friendships, remind them that their high school friends will always be special to them, but growing up and adulthood bring all sorts of new relationships that they will want to explore and nourish. And, winter break is right around the corner to reconnect with their older friends!

It's Not Too Late to Make Friends

Your student may feel like it's too late to get more connected on campus or that everyone else has already established their social circles, but the truth is friend groups are constantly evolving as students progress through their college experience. Following the COVID-19 pandemic and limited social interactions, many students have also been slower to engage and connect with their campus communities. Sometimes, continuing students feel like welcome weeks and semester kick-off activities hosted by the university are just for first-year students, but these events are designed to build connections and engagement for all students. Encourage your sophomore to participate. The second year is the perfect time to try something new—join a club, sign up for an intramural sports team, get a campus job, participate in fraternity or sorority recruitment, or attend a lecture on a topic of interest.

Living with Your Best Friend

During the first year, many students decide they want to live off campus in the upcoming year. Your student may want to live with a friend or group of friends. It's important to know this is not a requirement for a successful living arrangement. While students may be excited to live with friends, some of the most respectful and painless roommate experiences can be among non-friends with complementary habits and styles.

If your student decides to live with friends, there are many things to think about before move-in day. Students often develop deeper relationships when living with friends, but the arrangement can also present challenges. Sharing a space with anyone can be taxing on your relationship. It may be easier to take advantage of a roommate when they are also your friend. Multiple roommates means that several residents could side against another.

Often, leases for the upcoming school year are signed very early in the prior academic year. This can create a lot of pressure on students to find their roommates and secure the most desirable housing. Encourage your student to be proactive but not to rush into something they may regret. Before any lease is signed, there are many conversations to have with your student. Ask your student about their proposed roommates. Do they have similar social habits (e.g., early risers, party animals, smokers, drinkers)? Do they have similar expectations of cleanliness? Will they share food? Do they trust these individuals? Are they responsible students and community members?

Living with someone else is an adjustment, but a little reflection prior to committing can save a lot of frustration down the road.

Encourage your student and their roommates to set some ground rules prior to moving in together. Thinking about how to handle challenges and tensions can help everyone better navigate tricky situations if they come up. How will they maintain the common areas? When are quiet hours? How will they handle guests? What about overnight guests and romantic partners? How will you keep lines of communication open? Roommate groups should check in with each other often to ensure everyone is happy with their shared space.

Dating and Romantic Relationships

Just like friendships, romantic relationships evolve in the second year and beyond. Romantic relationships are an important part of our sense of belonging. College serves as a time to explore sexual identity and learn important lessons in intimacy and partnership. Some students even fall in love and meet their life partner in college.

Sophomore year can bring many changes to your student's relationships. Students who elected not to date in their first year may find themselves ready to explore in the second year. Students in a first-year relationship will either find it did not weather the summer break or feel like deepening the relationship this year. Others may choose not to date.

If your student does choose to date or commit to a relationship, talk to them about healthy partnerships. Remind them that, like friendships, romantic relationships have ups and downs and require a lot of effort to maintain. Relationships should be built on a foundation of honesty, trust, safety, and respect. Additionally, both partners should consent to being a part of the relationship and any sexual activities that may occur. That means each person involved has a clear understanding of what is happening, and they can change their mind at any time.

As your student's relationship status changes, you may also find yourself making adjustments. Your student may go to their partner for advice before seeking your guidance. Your student might wish to spend most of winter break at their partner's family home. Your student could announce that they want to move in together. As you navigate these new waters, open conversations with your student can help you manage expectations, share your point of view, and ask your student the reasons behind their decisions.

Supporting Healthy Romantic Relationships

Check in with your student about their dating life. Ask if they are dating anyone and ask questions about that person. It always feels good to have the support of a family member. Even if your student's choice is not exactly who you would have selected for them, it is important to remember it's *their* choice. Showing your support and maintaining open lines of communication can bring you even closer to your student. It also helps ensure that they feel comfortable talking with you about tougher topics like sex, contraceptives, and consent. And if they don't feel comfortable discussing these subjects with you, make sure they know what resources are available to them on campus (like the health offices).

Dating Violence and Abuse

Talk with your student about dating violence and abuse. There are many red flags for relationship violence that you and your student should know, including control, intimidation, disrespect, physical or sexual abuse, and lying. If your student ever experiences intimate or dating partner violence, there are many resources available on their campus (e.g., counseling services, wellness centers, sexual violence support programs) that can provide support and guidance.

Closing Advice

As your sophomore navigates their second year, they will naturally move toward more autonomy in their relationships. Remind them that you are still available to support them. You are hoping that your student feels a sense of belonging and connection on campus and that their friendships and romantic relationships are healthy and supportive of growth and success.

Conversation Starters

- What does it mean to you to be a good friend?
- How can you show up for your friends when they need support?
- Who are you thinking of living with next year? What do you have in common?
- What are some steps you and your roommates could take to establish a supportive and respectful living environment from the beginning?
- What new activities are you interested in exploring this year?
- How might you more deeply connect with a club or organization you joined last year?
- What are some qualities you look for in healthy romantic relationships? What might be a sign that a relationship is unhealthy?

Chapter 12
HOW FAR OFF CAMPUS IS THIS APARTMENT?

How to navigate choices about where to live

Marshall Greenleaf, Ed.D.
University of Massachusetts Lowell

Where to live can be one of the most stressful decisions your student makes when heading into their second year of college. Your student's next "home away from home" is going to be where they spend a significant amount of their time, and having a safe and comfortable living environment goes a long way toward helping your student be successful in school. Whether your student is wrestling with the decision of living on or off campus, or just starting the search for an off-campus apartment, there are ways you can prepare for and support a successful transition.

On-Campus versus Off-Campus Living

Living on campus offers your student opportunities to easily engage in activities and meet other students, while off-campus housing presents the opportunity for a more independent living experience. When entering into conversations with your student about this decision, it's important to talk through several key differences between the two options.

Cost

Cost is one of the primary driving factors behind the decision about where to live. It might be easy to look at the on-campus living price tag and assume that living off campus might be cheaper, but be sure your student is looking at *all* expenses. On-campus housing is an all-inclusive cost; one bill covers room, utilities, Wi-Fi, snow removal and upkeep of grounds, and often amenities like cable TV or streaming services. Encourage your student to list out all the anticipated costs of an off-campus apartment and compare that to the on-campus living cost.

Financial Aid

As part of determining housing costs, encourage your student to check with the financial aid office to see what the difference in aid would be for living on campus versus living off campus. Financial aid packages can fluctuate based on what your student is planning for their housing; be sure your student knows if their decision has any impact on their financial aid award.

Lease Length

Look at the length of any potential lease your student is signing. If your student is looking for housing during the academic year (typically September through May), what will they do with the additional months if they sign a 12-month lease for an off-campus apartment? These additional months should be factored into the overall cost of off-campus housing. If your student participates in a program such as study abroad that takes them away from campus, they will still be responsible for their off-campus lease. On-campus housing often does not always bill a student for time away from campus.

Neighbors

If your student decides to live on campus, they can be sure that every other person in their residence hall will also be a student. Deciding to live off campus means that your student will have neighbors from the surrounding community. This can be a great way to meet lots of different people, but it also comes with a responsibility for your student to be a good neighbor. They may need to be more mindful about things like noise or social gatherings when they are off campus. While their neighbors could be other students, there's no guarantee that this will be the case, and their new neighbors might well be on a different schedule than your college student.

Meals

On-campus living typically includes some sort of meal plan for your student to use in campus dining halls. If your student is used to having a wide variety of food available to them at all hours of the day, moving off campus and needing to make their own meals can feel like a huge transition. Your student might not be used to the responsibility of meal planning, shopping, and cooking their own food. Sometimes it can be tempting to get take-out from local restaurants which, while delicious, is not the most budget-conscious (or healthy) way to approach meals.

Roommates

Another decision your student will need to make, regardless of whether they live on or off campus, is whether they are going to have roommates. This might mean sharing a bedroom or having a single bedroom in a shared apartment. Either way, good communication regarding expectations for a shared living environment is crucial, even if your student is planning on living with a friend. Your student should discuss aspects of day-to-day life, such as the level of cleanliness expected, noise levels, what items can be shared, and what's okay in terms of guests and visitors. Many colleges offer a roommate agreement form that your student can fill out to help make discussing these preferences with their future roommate easier. Your student might feel awkward about having these conversations, but they will decrease the likelihood of any roommate issues in the future.

So, what happens if roommate issues do arise? If your student is living on campus, residence life staff are typically available to help mediate the situation. If that doesn't work, there's usually the opportunity for your student to change rooms. Neither of these are an option if your student is living off campus and has signed a lease. If a roommate issue occurs, your student will be responsible for working with their roommate to figure out a solution. It's important that your student be direct in their communication about the issue and solution-oriented in figuring out how to resolve it. Is there a way for the roommates to compromise? Are there small adjustments each roommate could make to help improve the situation? Does everyone in the apartment need to create a cleaning schedule? If your student needs help with these conversations, is there a neutral third party who could assist?

Preparing for the Off-Campus Housing Search

If your student decides that living off campus is the right choice, there are ways that they can prepare in order to be successful in their housing search.

Create a Budget

Your student needs to have a realistic idea of how much they are able to spend on their housing each month. A good place to start is to add up all of their ongoing monthly expenses. This should include everything your student will need money for and can also include academic expenses (e.g., fees, books, supplies): rent, utilities, internet, groceries, transportation, clothes, meals out, and entertainment. Next, have your student list out income that is coming in each month (including any family contributions that you might be making). Compare the two lists, and be sure to add some wiggle room for emergencies. This will help determine what amount your student is able to pay for rent.

Check Out Campus Resources

Many colleges and universities have an office dedicated to supporting students living off campus. These offices may have listings of available off-campus housing and often have educational resources about searching for housing and signing a lease. Roommate-matching services might be offered, as well. Encourage your student to check out the resources available to them and reach out to staff if they have any questions. It can also be a good idea to look at town or city online resources for renters, including ordinances, policies, and tenant rights. Your student may want to check out local real estate agents who specialize in apartment rentals.

Make a List

It can be helpful to have your student make a list of priorities focused on what they need from their housing. Does it need to be within a certain distance to campus? Does parking need to be available, and if so, is there an additional cost? Is it close to campus transportation? Are there specific amenities (e.g., laundry, gym, off-street parking) your student is looking for? It's important that your student think through what they need from a living space but also that they be realistic and flexible. Help them think about what is a necessity versus a want. This can help narrow the search down to specific areas.

Signing a Lease

This might sound like common sense, but, if possible, your student should tour the apartment or living space prior to signing a lease. When this might not be possible—if your student is studying abroad, for example—they should do their due diligence in finding out as much information as possible about their potential future home. Do they have friends who could tour the property? Could you tour the property for them? Are there reviews of the apartment online? Your student should go into signing the lease feeling as confident as possible about their choice of living arrangements for sophomore year.

Before your student signs a lease, they should feel clear about their responsibilities as tenants and about what is provided by the property owner. Some of the basic facts include when the rent is due, how the rent is paid, how repairs and maintenance requests work, what (if any) utilities are included, and whether subletting is allowed. Your student should feel comfortable with all aspects of their future rental before signing the lease. Your student might also consider getting rental insurance in order to provide financial compensation for their belongings should anything happen to the property, such as theft or fire. Some property owners require rental insurance as part of the lease.

Closing Advice

Searching for an off-campus apartment can be a great opportunity for your student to build life skills for the future, but the task may feel scary or uncomfortable. You can offer support to your student as they approach this milestone by:

- Visiting potential apartments together
- Offering to cosign the lease (some properties might even require this for first-time student renters)

- Helping construct your student's budget
- Listening and offering advice throughout the process
- Helping pick supplies and decor for the new space

Your student will need—and want—your guidance during this time.

Conversation Starters

- Have you thought about where you might want to live next year? Do you have a place in mind?
- How will you get to campus?
- What can I do to help with your housing search?
- What is your budget for housing expenses?
- Do you know who you want to live with? Where will your friends be living?

Chapter 13
WHAT IF SOMETHING GOES WRONG?

How to respond to personal or campus-wide emergencies

Chelsea Petree, Ph.D.
Rochester Institute of Technology

No matter how much you plan and prepare, things will go wrong, whether it's a bad grade, an illness, or a campus or community crisis (as if you weren't worried enough!). It's always hard to hear your student is struggling or in trouble. The most important thing to remember in a crisis—no matter the size—is to stay calm. Your student will need your support and guidance and is more likely to come to you with a personal issue if they know you won't be mad or judge and are there to listen and assist.

How a university communicates with parents will depend on whether it's a personal crisis or a campus/community emergency, as well as the scope of the emergency. In order to make sure you get all information available, sign up for all parent email lists, follow the university on social media, and make sure your student adds an emergency contact to their university account.

Personal Crises

The previous chapters have given you insight into the types of issues that might arise with your student. Personal crises can include a bad grade, a decision to withdraw or take a leave of absence, illness, mental health issues such as anxiety, or a breakup. In any situation, it will be difficult to hear that something went wrong, especially if you are far away. As you also have read, FERPA and HIPAA prohibit colleges from sharing information with parents, even in the case of most medical emergencies.

If your student becomes ill, please remember that campus health centers have limitations on what support they can provide. The student health fee will not cover transportation to an emergency room or outside care, although the health center may have resources to help students find appropriate care. Understanding what the campus health system provides in advance will help when an emergency arises.

In the area of academics, parents will not be notified if a student is failing, not attending class, or withdrawing from courses, all of which can seem like an emergency if you see an F on their final grades. More commonly, you will hear from your student that something is wrong, hopefully before it becomes an emergency.

If your student calls you in a panic, consider the following:

- *Is this an emergency?* What sounds like an emergency in the heat of the moment might not actually be an urgent situation. One failed class does not mean your student is failing at college. A bout of food poisoning does not mean your student cannot eat on campus ever again. Parents are likely to get calls when emotions are high. In most cases, it's best to let yourself and your student calm down before jumping to conclusions.

- *How can I help my student clarify the issue?* You hear about the problem, but what's often more important is what is at the root of the problem. For example, a class that is "too hard" might actually be a call to learn new study skills and habits. Asking open-ended questions and digging deeper will help you learn what is really going on, which is necessary for finding the right solution.
- *Might they be exaggerating?* It's not that your student is lying to you, it's that they are afraid of getting into trouble (yes, even as a young adult, they don't want their parents upset with them!). They also want you on their side and may bend the truth to get you there (e.g., if they say they've reached out to their advisor over and over again…it might be once, late at night, the day before the exam). This is completely normal for this stage of student and adult development, and nothing to get upset about. It is important, though, to keep this in mind when working with your student, especially if you end up talking to university staff.
- *How can I guide them to take control of the situation?* When your student calls in a panic, your gut reaction will be to step in and take care of it or find answers. Your student might even ask you to make the call for them. Only in very rare cases should you take over. Rather, empower your student to take the lead by helping them talk through the issues and think of solutions.
- *What are your student's strengths and how can they use them in this situation?* If your student is in a panic, they might forget that they have the skills needed to move forward. Reminders of previous times they have problem-solved can go a long way in building confidence and resilience.
- *What office can I refer them to?* As you've learned in this book, there are offices on campus for just about everything

and many support resources for students. You may remember something you heard at orientation or read in a parent newsletter that can help your student. A simple online search can go a long way as well. Helping in this way will take a little stress off your student while still allowing them to do the heavy lifting.

- *How can I partner with the university?* If you do have to call to either clarify policies and procedures or help your student find resources, remember that staff will continue to refer to what your student needs to do. It is often a good idea to include students on those calls or emails so everyone receives the same information and is on the same page. (Remember the first question in this list and wait to call until all parties are calm and can have a reasonable and productive discussion.)

Campus Emergencies

A campus emergency, such as a health outbreak, power outage, extreme weather, or a high-profile death, can be scarier than a personal crisis, especially if you hear it from the news or university communications before you hear from your student. When you talk to your student about this level of emergency, make sure that they are okay without alarming them. Ask if they are connected to emergency communication notices sent by their college, including emails, texts, and phone calls so they can stay up to date on plans and directions. Universities may or may not send information about campus-wide emergencies directly to parents. If your student's university doesn't, stay connected on social media and watch websites for information on emergencies and procedures.

Most universities have an emergency response team that has plans in place for crises. It can be hard to know everything you need to plan for until you're in it, though, so understand that it can take time to fix the issue if, for example, a sudden windstorm knocks the power out in the dorms. In any campus emergency, there is likely a large number of staff working around the clock to support students, from finding alternative housing, providing mental health resources, and working with the local community to provide resources. Trust that they are not only working as quickly as they can but finding appropriate solutions for the scale of the emergency.

The suggestions above for working through a personal crisis can also be useful when communicating with your student about a larger-scale emergency. You will want, for example, to know if your student is personally impacted. If not, it is most helpful to keep the university communication channels open for students and families who need immediate assistance. As noted above, students can sometimes make emergencies sound worse than they truly are. For example, you may not have heard about the campus-wide "outbreak" of food poisoning because only a tiny percentage of students became sick. While you will be frustrated if this happened to your student and you weren't informed, the university will not want to cause unnecessary, mass panic in parents for smaller-scale issues.

Closing Advice

Even though emotions will be high in the case of an emergency, it's important to remain calm. In the case of a personal crisis, remind your student of campus resources and encourage them to seek help. Trust that the university always has students' best interests in mind and will work quickly to provide support and assistance.

Conversation Starters

- How does your college communicate to students about emergency situations?
- Do you follow your university on social media so you can stay informed on what's happening?
- How can I best support you if you are struggling?
- Where would you find support if you were feeling overwhelmed?
- What steps will you take if you notice your grades are dropping?
- Let's set aside some time to create a plan of action if there ever was an emergency.

Chapter 14
IS MY STUDENT JUNIOR READY?

How to prepare for next year

Lindsey Bray
Cornell University

As your student advances in their educational journey, issues that once caused concern often feel easy and practiced as you and your student have worked through them, but new concerns may take their place. As your student progresses through their second year, they have learned the basics of college. They have found a friend group and hopefully feel a sense of belonging and connection with their school, classmates, faculty, and staff. But looking ahead to junior year, they may face new challenges as they progress in their major, study abroad, and work on finding a balance between school and life. This chapter will help you think about what's next in their college journey.

Classroom Challenges

Your student will continue to be challenged as they advance on their academic journey. They will explore new concepts and work more closely with faculty members. Entering their upper-level classes will challenge and test their ideas, and how they are asked to demonstrate their knowledge will change. While first- and second-year students become accustomed to tests or quizzes requiring memorization, many upper-level classes require students to apply their knowledge through more extensive writing or in a practice setting. This may mean students need to change how they study, take notes, or use their time outside the classroom. Students can use the writing center, tutoring, or learning strategies center to assist them. If your student feels challenged, you may want to help by asking:

- Have you reached out to your professor or gone to their office hours to get extra help?
- Is there tutoring available in this subject?
- Do you have a classmate who could help you study?
- Do you need to implement some new study strategies or spend more time on this class?

Career Exploration

Some students arrive at college knowing exactly what they want to study, while others are ready to explore. Those arriving with certainty about their studies may also decide to explore new topics.

During their sophomore year, students are often required to choose their major, which will help them begin to narrow their thoughts on a future career. While some majors, such as engineering or nursing, may have a direct path to a career, many others hold an array of possibilities. Your student should use their career services office to help them narrow down their interests and explore career options. Students have access to resources that can evaluate their skills and interests to suggest opportunities and careers they may not be familiar with. College is a time for your student to explore their interests and find an area in which they are passionate about learning. This passion can help lead to a future career. While having a plan for after graduation is important, students will find that most majors provide essential skills and knowledge that can be applied to a variety of jobs in different industries. Some students may know exactly what they want to do when they graduate, while some may not. What is most important is that they use their education, interests, and the resources available to them to provide them access to future career opportunities.

As students are challenged, they may question their major or career ideas. If your student is not doing as well as expected in the required classes for their major or is less interested in this material than they expected to be, this is the time for them to reflect on their choice. You may have encouraged your student's future career vision, but if they're interested in making a change, listen to why they feel the original choice no longer fits them. Support them as they work through the decision. Your student may feel as though they are disappointing you by making this change and will want your validation and support.

It may seem concerning if your student makes a major change in their studies, but it is not uncommon for students to use their time in college to explore new topics. Many classes can transfer between majors, but students should talk with their advisors when thinking about a change. Many institutions have systems within the student portal that show how current credits can apply to a new major. Here are some things to discuss with your student as they consider a change in major:

- What inspired your change? Did you take an elective in this area?
- Have you talked with your advisor about the change?
- How will this affect your graduation plan?
- How does this change your plans for after graduation? Are you interested in going to graduate school or directly to a job?

Internships and job shadowing are useful ways to explore potential careers. They provide a chance to explore the facets of a job, workplace, and environment. They can be an important way for your student to learn more about what a job entails. Internships can span a semester or multiple years. They often are completed for credit. Job shadowing is a chance for a student to follow a professional for a day or a few hours and would not be for credit. Both opportunities help a student build their network of professionals who can provide letters of recommendation for a job or graduate school, job referrals, and future opportunities. Students should be actively building their network throughout college through their classmates, faculty, staff, and coworkers. These connections will be invaluable while in college and beyond.

Balance

As your student looks to their junior year, they may be interested in becoming a leader in an organization they have been active in. Involvement in campus activities and leadership roles can help your student learn crucial interpersonal skills highly valued by employers. But as students juggle their increasingly difficult studies and the additional demands of their activities, some may struggle to find a balance. If cocurricular activities feel more engaging and fun as students work alongside their friends, they may find themselves putting outside-the-classroom activities ahead of their schoolwork. Taking on too much can also lead to burnout and a lack of motivation.

Encourage your student to:

- Take time for themselves. Find a space that recharges them. Maybe it is a walking trail off campus, their favorite coffee shop, or working out at the gym.
- Find a balance. This is a lifelong quest, and it is important to be aware of it from an early age.

- Identify their triggers for burnout and recognize early when they have to say no to an opportunity or take a step back in order to focus on and care for themselves.

As students balance their time between classes and extracurricular activities, they may also be balancing it with a significant other. This may be someone they met their first year or an intense, newer relationship. This relationship can create happiness for your student but also requires another level of balancing. Your student and their partner should be supporting each other, but if one student is in a more intense program, the other person may not fully understand what time commitment is required from their partner. Encourage your student to explain their responsibilities to their partner so the pair can try to balance school and relationship. Often, spending quality time together can help to ease the tension as they create connection.

Studying Abroad

Many students use their junior year to study abroad. When else in your life can you put everything on hold and to go live in a different country for several months? Many parents may be worried about their student studying abroad, as this may be the first time the student has left the country or traveled alone. The cost of studying abroad also often concerns parents. Most schools offer additional scholarships for students to study abroad and allow their current scholarships to apply toward the cost as well. Studying abroad is much more than a trip to another country; it is an opportunity for your student to immerse themselves in a different culture in a way that is often impossible on a shorter trip. They will also use this time to see different perspectives as they learn with native students and those from different colleges.

As you help your student prepare to study abroad, think about their transition to college last year. Did they get homesick? Did they embrace their new independence? How did they adapt to change? If your student adapted to college, made friends easily, and was rarely homesick, your student may need less support while they are away. But if they had a more challenging time adjusting, studying abroad may be hard for them as they leave their friends and routines to explore a new place. Encourage your student to connect early with the study abroad office to meet classmates who will be on the trip. They can also ask to be connected with a student who recently returned who might have suggestions.

The study abroad office will have resources on essential aspects of travel, such as costs, insurance, and visas. Students will need to understand what is provided with their experience and what they are responsible for. A few things to consider:

- Will they be living in university housing, or will they need to secure a local residence?
- What are the transportation options?
- How will they use their cell phone? Will changes be needed for the current phone plan or will a new one be needed when they arrive?
- Is additional health insurance needed? How does your current plan apply?

See Chapter 5 for more about study abroad.

Closing Advice

Your student continues to grow. This year will bring new challenges, but they are challenges that will help them to mature and learn for the future. Continue to support them, but understand that as they grow, your support may also need to change as your relationship shifts to that of a mentor.

Continued Conversations

- Have your classes changed your thoughts about your future career? What new interests have you found?
- Are you still on track to graduate when expected?
- How are you prioritizing self-care? What are some ways that you are finding time to relax and recharge?
- Have you taken time to talk to your partner about balancing your personal and college lives? What are some challenges you may both be facing?
- Where are you thinking about studying abroad? What kinds of programs are offered? How long will you travel?

Conclusion

Sophomore year lays the groundwork for the next few years and what lies beyond the diploma. While there are potential concerns to consider, this can be one of the most exciting years for your college student. Choosing a major, getting a taste of independent living, and becoming more deeply engaged in a beloved student organization are just a few of the many exciting experiences they can have this year.

As the stakes get higher, so may the pull to step in and fix things for your student. Remember, however, that there are valuable lessons to be learned from mistakes and setbacks. The ways in which your sophomore picks themselves back up after failing a test, breaking up with a significant other, or losing a campus job creates the resilience necessary to get through life's challenges. The good news is that these lessons are happening in a place with a wide safety net. Trust the campus resources and encourage your student to learn and grow from negative experiences.

No matter how significant the changes this year, your college sophomore is still your child deep down, and they're doing exactly what you taught them to do: explore, learn, and grow. Be proud of them—and of yourself.

www.ingramcontent.com/pod-product-compliance
Lightning Source LLC
Chambersburg PA
CBHW011758040426
42446CB00018B/3454